SAINT MUNGO'S CITY

A Novel

By SARAH TYTLER
AUTHOR OF 'THE BRIDE'S PASS,' 'WHAT SHE CAME THROUGH,
'BEAUTY AND THE BEAST,' ETC.

IN THREE VOLUMES
VOL. III.

London
CHATTO AND WINDUS, PI(
1884
[*All rights reserved*]

This scarce antiquarian book is included in our special *Legacy Reprint Series*. In the interest of creating a more extensive selection of rare historical book reprints, we have chosen to reproduce this title even though it may possibly have occasional imperfections such as missing and blurred pages, missing text, poor pictures, markings, dark backgrounds and other reproduction issues beyond our control. Because this work is culturally important, we have made it available as a part of our commitment to protecting, preserving and promoting the world's literature. Thank you for your understanding.

CONTENTS OF VOL. III.

CHAPTER		PAGE
XXVII.	THE MISS MACKINNONS' HARMONIOUS LITTLE ARRANGEMENT	1
XXVIII.	THE OFFICERS OF JUSTICE IN ST. MUNGO'S SQUARE—CLARIBEL DRYSDALE STANDS BY HER COLOURS	19
XXIX.	'LOVE WILL VENTURE IN WHERE WISDOM AINCE HAS BEEN'	40
XXX.	A HORRIBLE SUSPICION ASSAILS AULD TAM	58
XXXI.	THE SUSPICION BECOMES A CERTAINTY	84
XXXII.	IN THE BALANCE	111
XXXIII.	A DROWNING MAN'S STRAWS	128
XXXIV.	AULD TAM 'FEY'	150

CONTENTS.

CHAPTER		PAGE
XXXV.	SIR HUGO LAYS HIMSELF AND WILLOUGHBY COURT AT YOUNG EPPIE'S FEET	180
XXXVI.	THE SEAL TO SIR HUGO'S SUIT	201
XXXVII.	A CHARMED SAIL	216
XXXVIII.	THE LAST OF RORY OF THE SHELTIES—DR. PETER ON THE SCENT	248
XXXIX.	THE SACRIFICE	263
XL.	A NEW CALCULATION	292
XLI.	ATHOLE MURRAY SKETCHES A MODERN FUGGEREI—THE MISS MACKINNONS' ULTIMATUM	317

SAINT MUNGO'S CITY.

CHAPTER XXVII.

THE MISS MACKINNONS' HARMONIOUS LITTLE ARRANGEMENT.

To begin with, something closed the Miss Mackinnons' lips on this point, and not a word was said among them of the defrauding of Miss Mackinnon and Miss Janet to enrich Miss Bethia, sitting with downcast eyes, wringing the hands hidden in her lap.

At last Miss Janet said, not so much bitterly as with forced gaiety:

'You are up in the buckle [exalted], Betheye—an heiress; you'll no be speaking to me and Meye.'

'Oh, Janet!' burst out Miss Bethia, breaking down and sobbing with mingled pain and shame. 'Do you think I would touch the money? I'll gie it back, every penny, to you and Meye, the moment I've got it into my fingers.'

'But there's twa and whiles three at a bargain-making,' said Miss Janet, with wounded pride in her voice. 'Do you think we would tak' from anither—though she happened to be our sister—what was ours, but had been wulled awa' from us?'

'But that would be cruel!' protested Miss Bethia, in still greater distress. 'How could I help it? An ill-kinded man! Gude guide us!' pausing in horror; 'to think that I should speak ill of him, and him hardly in the mools. But I never set een on him, never.'

'You gowk, what does that signify?' Miss Janet was provoked into treating the heiress with little courtesy.

'What ails her?' cried Miss Mackinnon wrathfully. 'Is she pretendin' to greet for the man, now that he has left her the maist of his money? I cannot stand such hypocrisy.'

Miss Bethia wept on, regardless of the good fortune, which was misfortune to her, and equally unrestrained by the manner in which her sorrow was misunderstood.

'What can I do?' she lamented. 'I never wanted your shares; I never thocht money would come between me and you and Meye.'

Miss Janet was a little softened.

'You can do nothing—as long as the paper stands, the money's yours. But we're no blaming you, save for being silly —and we'll tak' the will for the deed.'

'Oh, thank you! thank you, Janet!' said Miss Bethia gratefully. 'If only Meye and you will not tak' me for a traitor and hypocrite—and me never to have seen the man! —I'll no mind so muckle. But is there no way to gie back the money, and share and share alike as we should have done? Why can I not do as I like with my ain, as he did?'

'You're fast enough with your ain,' said Miss Janet, in fresh displeasure. 'It has not been yours mair than an hour. I'll tell you what, Betheye,' the speaker relapsed into a sardonic mood, 'it's a' very weel to say what you'll do or not do the noo; but it's as likely as not that the word o' the sillar will bring some fair-spoken blackguard of a man after you. You'll marry him fast; then Meye and me will be left in the lurch, and he'll help you to spend the money that should have been ours.'

'Never!' declared Miss Bethia; and she failed to simper as of old, but a dull-red rose in her lined face and spread over it. She had, as she would have said, given up all thought of a man for many a day; but mercenary as were the notions attributed to this man, the sudden revival of the vision brought a shy, guilty sense of gratification, which the next moment covered poor Miss Bethia with confusion and remorse. Would she sacrifice her sisters even for the best man that ever breathed? 'I wonder at you, Janet!' she said, so vehemently that there was a suspicion of weakness and fear in the vehemence; 'an auld maid like me.'

'There's nae fules like old anes,' said Miss Janet jauntily; 'and you'll cease to be an auld maid when the scamp has made you a young wife. Ye ken you'll be young among the mawtrons, though you're auld among the maidens.'

'It's cruel,' repeated Miss Bethia, with an ominous intensity of distress in the kindling fire of temptation. 'Oh! I wish I had the horrible money to fling it into the fire, or cast it into Clyde.'

'What good would that do?' demanded the matter-of-fact Miss Janet, 'unless you wanted him to loup in and fish it out.'

Miss Bethia groaned.

'Stop her greetin',' broke in Miss Mackinnon, in greater disgust than before. 'I canna bide sic false pretences, Betheye; it's like haudin' an ingan [onion] to your een. Hoo can ye try sic a trick upon Janet and me?'

'I wull greet,' Miss Bethia suddenly turned upon her sisters; 'I have cause to greet. I thocht my ain sisters liked and trusted me, and I was prood to slave wi' them and for them; but I find I was mista'en when they're ready to misdoubt me, for nae faut o' mine, and to tant me because of the wrongdoing of another.'

Miss Janet was taken aback by this new attitude of Miss Bethia, and the feelings reflected on her face were quickly caught up by her elder sister. They both paused, irresolute what to say next.

'We dinna misdoubt you, Betheye,' said Miss Janet, in a more subdued tone. 'But you maun grant this has been a shock as well as a hardship to us—the younger to be served out of the elders' portions—the elder to be dependent on the younger's generosity, or whatever you like to ca't.'

'Oh, it is maist abominable!' admitted Miss Bethia, with all her heart. 'But it is no generosity—it's justice which ocht to be done; and surely I'll be helped to do't, though I've to get the Queen to back me.'

'It's an expensive road to the Queen, though her Majesty is very gude and kind,' said Miss Janet, not affording any encouragement to the scheme, but refraining from the strong derision she had been practising. The next moment she added: 'I think there may be an easier plan—it has just flashed upon me—if you're in earnest, Betheye, as I do not question.'

'Try me,' said Miss Bethia, with trembling eagerness.

'Weel, I apprehend there's just this parchment binding you doon—I said, as long as the paper stands we've but to submit. But what is to hinder us from making awa' wi't? The wull concerns nane but oorsel's and the servants—that dour, sly jaud of a housekeeper and her man. We are perfectly agreed, and we can easily settle wi' servants; we'll pay them every bawbee of their legacy, though it's twice as muckle as it need have been—and that is all they'll care for. What need is there to keep the paper and fash our heads with it? We'll tear it up, and think nae mair o't, while we divide Jean Mackinnon's money fair among oorsel's.'

'The very thing,' said Miss Bethia, with a great sigh of relief and of lurking regret that the legacy had not been ten thousand or ten hundred. In that case, even the third fraction of it might have constituted her an heiress, with all an heiress's privileges and trials. She might have been courted, she might have needed to stand firm, to decline to be wooed, to give her suitors a dignified yet amiable dismissal. There was glamour in the prospect, but it was not for Miss Bethia. 'To destroy the wull,' she hammered on at Miss Janet's project, 'which deals just with the servants, to whom we can make their legacy gude, while we are fully agreed on a fresh division of Jean Mackinnon's money, is so easy and natural. I wonder it did not occur to us at aince. Let us do it this minute, Janet, before Mr. Mair or ony of the gentlemen come back.' Miss Bethia was opposed to the least delay. 'Shall I tak' out the paper and tear it?' she cried.

'On second thochts, it had better be brunt, and then there will be no trouble with the fragments,' said Miss Janet, gratified with having been the originator of a good idea, and full of importance in putting it into execution. 'I believe I have heard,' continued Miss Janet dogmatically, 'that, when a wull is brunt in this way, the parties interested stand round a can'le, and each holds a corner of the dockiment over the lowe, so as to mak' sure they're all consenting to the destruction; then if any wyte [blame] is incurred, it will fa' on all alike.'

'But is there ony fear o' wyte?' asked Miss Bethia, startled. 'Maybe, after a', we had better wait and ask Mr. Mair.'

'Maybe, after a', we had better let the wull stand,' said Miss Janet scornfully, for the resource hit upon had by this time recommended itself thoroughly to her. It would restore her own and Miss Mackinnon's birthright, by the curl of a flame, if not by the stroke of a pen, and thus immediately wipe out the insult and loss inflicted upon them. And the act would prevent any danger of Miss Bethia's wavering in her design, or being overborne by the arguments of others.

Not only was the plan Miss Janet's, and therefore right in her eyes; she was proud of it, and sought to keep it in her own possession, and carry it out independently for herself and her sisters. She enjoyed the notion of astonishing and discomfiting Mr. Mair by her sharpness and promptitude. In fact, Miss Janet had got out her head, and was bent on 'running her own road.'

'You ken I did not mean to let the wull stand,' said Miss Bethia, hurt, and reproachful. 'But you'll speak to Mr. Mair after. You'll tell him what you've done with the wull he gave up to you.'

'I'll speak to Mair when he speaks to

me,' said Miss Janet, full of refractoriness.
'What has he, ony mair than his clerk, to do with Fenton of Strathdivie's wull, that was made on our account? Mair drew it up, as ony ither writer micht have done; but it was not his wull, or yours either, Betheye, as ane micht think, to hear ye speak. You've sune learnt to tak' a great deal upon you. You seem to forget, because you've been preferred without reason, that we're your elders, and Meye's the head of the hoose.'

'I dinna forget,' said Miss Bethia, with a full heart.

Miss Janet went on harshly:

'If you're in earnest in makin' reparation by being willin' to join Meye and me, in what we've had cause to suppose you had fixed to do, ye'll say no more about it.'

Miss Bethia said no more.

When it was put to Miss Mackinnon whether she would support her sisters in their spirited measure, she replied with hoarse emphasis, 'Certainly !' and looked about for a matchbox.

There was a wax taper by the inkstand, and Miss Janet was in such a hurry that she would not wait to ring for a candle, though it seemed doubtful at the first glance whether the little light could effectually consume the two or three broad-margined, widely-written, crackling pages of which the will was composed.

'We'll tak' it leaf by leaf,' said Miss Janet methodically. 'There are only three o' us; but I'll haud twa corners, while you and Meye can tak' the other twa, ane each.'

The process was a slow one. Miss Janet and Miss Mackinnon stood unflinchingly, braving the little wreaths of smoke which seemed to rise out of all proportion to the performance, even daring the yellow tongues of flame that darted across the paper, and threatened the bony fingers.

Miss Bethia shook fitfully, disturbing the balance of the arrangement, and shrank nervously from the burning, as if it had been Archie Fenton putting forth fiery fingers to execute vengeance upon her for her contemptuous treatment of his will.

The whole fantastic incident—witnessed under the solemn splendour of a moorland sunset, which shone in through a western window; the three big, gaunt, hard-featured old women, in more or less fixed theatrically tragic attitudes, the right hand extended, grasping the sheet of paper; Miss Janet's dauntless, impassive face; Miss Mackinnon's glittering, restless eyes, lit up by an imprisoned spirit; Miss Bethia's features working with anxiety and dread; the shrivelling, blackening paper; the jets of flame, the smoke—all bore a marvellous, grotesque resemblance to the witches' incantations of the Middle Ages. Fenton of Strathdivie's will might have been one of those bonds, written in letters of blood, that sold souls to the foul fiend, and could no more be burnt in fire, which was their natural element, than the devil could perish in his own hell.

Towards the close of the strange proceeding there was a slight creaking of the door and rustling of something behind it, which caused Miss Bethia to look round in fresh terror; but the trifling noise ceased almost instantly. The charred fragments of the will dropped on the floor, and were carefully collected by Miss Janet in the fire-shovel and deposited in the empty grate. Another match was lit and applied to them, and she was soon warranted in the triumphant announcement:

'There's naethin' left but white aiss [ashes], let Mair or wha like mak' what they can oot o't. We've snapped our fingers at Fenton o' Strathdivie, in what was his ain hoose, too.'

'Oh! wheesht, Janet, wheesht!' implored the appalled Miss Bethia.

But Miss Janet did not heed her younger sister.

'We're free to do what we like wi' our ain,' she proclaimed exultingly.

Indeed, the Miss Mackinnons were not

disturbed in their harmonious little arrangement, either on that night or before their departure next morning.

Mr. Mair, in his character of host, sat later over the funeral dinner than was prudent, with regard to catching the train by which he could reach that night the bosom of his family, in the market-town where he practised as a solicitor. He left in such a hurry that he declined a parting interview with Mrs. Todd, and contented himself with sending his clerk to fetch the desk from the study, and take leave for him of the Miss Mackinnons. Indeed, Mr. Mair had not been very favourably impressed by the ladies. He considered rightly that he had done all in his power for their comfort, and as a poor return, he had been forced to bear a considerable amount of rudeness from Miss Janet. He was a long-suffering man, but endurance has its limits.

The ladies, on their part, had not thought of leaving Strathdivie the very day after the funeral, but had rather meditated an indefinite stay—a sort of taking possession till their claims were settled, with the deliberate investigation of that ' stoucherie ' [collection of goods in an old family house], all or part of which they had fondly hoped would have fallen to their share. But the sisters were compelled to understand that the place and everything it contained belonged to the late owner's New Zealand cousins, among whose property the women had no excuse for prowling, however natural their regretful curiosity. At the same time they had every reason to distrust any prolonged civilities from Mrs. Todd, the housekeeper, who was again mistress of the situation, having been appointed by the lawyer to continue in her former place till the term should bring a new tenant to the old house.

And Miss Janet, in spite of her supreme confidence in her own powers, was a little doubtful what step to take next in the acquirement of the money, the division of which she had already altered in a summary fashion. It might be necessary for the sisters again to have that respectable family adjunct—a man of business; and if so, the sooner they applied to him the better on all these counts. Miss Janet and Miss Mackinnon filled Miss Bethia's heart with thankfulness, by deciding to quit Strathdivie the following forenoon.

But another person was before the Miss Mackinnons. Mrs. Todd, in her new mourning, accompanied by her canny lout of a husband, in his Sunday suit, had slipped out of the house, leaving a deputy in charge, by break of day. Ten minutes afterwards, the late Fenton of Strathdivie's confidential servant might have been seen at the little railway station, starting on a journey by the early Parliamentary train.

In the course of the day, Mr. Mair appeared again on the scene—not coming quietly by train this time, but driving in hot haste across the country, arriving at Strathdivie to find the birds flown, if he came in search of the Miss Mackinnons, who had departed for Glasgow a quarter of an hour before. The lawyer was in an excited, disturbed frame of mind when he heard that the ladies were gone. He turned the head of his reeking horse without giving it either rest or refreshment, saying to himself:

'There is nothing for it but an application to the fiscal; and I doubt if I'll come out clear in the business. I should not have been so careless; but who would have thought the old beldames were capable of such a trick? But, good Heavens! to think what will be the upshot, and how the wretched old women will be served for their desperate deed!'

CHAPTER XXVIII.

THE OFFICERS OF JUSTICE IN ST. MUNGO'S SQUARE — CLARIBEL DRYSDALE STANDS BY HER COLOURS.

THE Miss Mackinnons, arriving at home towards the close of the day, required more than the following night's rest to restore them to their normal condition. They felt as if they had gone on a long and perilous expedition, and encountered many exciting adventures. The journey had not been altogether fruitless, and there was at the end of it that happy restoration to the grey old house in St. Mungo's Square, which caused Miss Bethia to cry out fondly, 'Eh! hame is kindly,' and Miss Janet to sniff the thick air as if it were her own special property. She gloried in the reek. Still, it could not be expected that the travellers would at once master the shocks and fatigue of so unusual an experience. The ladies were not in trim for visitors, which was unfortunate, since they had for their share that day, not only the Lieutenant, who had started from Oban on hearing the news of Fenton of Strathdivie's death, but, of all people in the world, Claribel Drysdale.

Clary had come up to town from Lochgoilhead, unattended by any other member of the family except young Tam, on his way to his office. She had meant to do a little shopping, remain for the night in the house of friends of the Drysdales, and sail back again next day. She had taken it into her head, for some reasons known only to herself, to call, for the first time in her life, on the Miss Mackinnons, knowing nothing of their recent absence, or, for that matter, of Fenton of Strathdivie, and believing Eneas Mackinnon to be still with the Semples at Oban. Could it be that Clary, so calm and cool and sufficient for herself in all circumstances, had simply pined for her absent lover, who was not to be thought of as a husband for her, and, yearning to have tidings of him, had suddenly conceived the idea of calling on his old grand-aunts, the indigent gentlewomen who were her father's *protégées*?

Anyhow, there was Claribel behaving herself very graciously, looking a wonderful specimen of youth and beauty, in an expensively quiet and suitable walking-dress; a hat with hardly any trimming, from Paris; sober gloves and boots, also from Paris; a little exquisite embroidery on the collar and cuffs of her gown. She formed a striking figure among the others in the dull, dingy room, and won golden opinions from its usual occupants. Yet one would have thought that Claribel, with her natural and acquired elegance, was too well regulated a person in everything, had too high and at the same time too conventional a standard to meet the Miss Mackinnons' views; that she would not be smart or bouncing, or, on the other hand, deferential enough for those her seniors. However, they were paying her homage not merely with ulterior motives on their grand-nephew's account, or because of some regard for what her father, Tam Drysdale, had done for them first and last. It was principally because this well-assured, courteous, composed example of maidenhood—maidenhood among the upstart, wealthy, influential 'dirt' of modern trade, that Miss Janet was wont to despise —took the old lady by surprise—took away her breath in some occult manner, and rendered her nearly subdued, and almost well-bred.

There was Eneas, by far the most uncomfortable of the party, in some degree consoled by what in its turn amazed him —that is to say, the unexpectedly commonplace civility of his kinswomen.

Neither could the Lieutenant altogether resist a throb of what he knew, at the bottom of his heart, to be idiotic hope occasioned by Claribel's voluntary uninvited presence in St. Mungo's Square—Claribel with her innate refinement and dignity, sitting apparently happy, and at her ease, among his queer, plain old aunts. Was it for his sake? Could it be for his sake? Yet, if it were so, how could he—penniless, without the most distant prospect of rising to any purpose in his profession—propose to accept gratefully, and repay richly, such rare generous devotion?

A ring at the door-bell—not loud, but prolonged, as if delivered from weighty considerations—startled the party, and Miss Bethia vanished to perform the office of the servant who had never been replaced.

'Tradesmen are very forward and pushing for orders,' remarked Miss Janet. 'Does not your mammaw find it so, Miss Drysdale?'

'Well, we're rather out of the way of shop-boys in the country; and my mother is so fond of marketing when she gets the opportunity, that she never complains,' answered Clary, with a pleasant laugh.

At that moment Miss Bethia looked in with a face grown pale, a dazed look, and a paper in her hand.

'Will you come here and speak, Eneas?'

She summoned him mysteriously. He rose slowly to grant her request.

'What is't, Betheye? Speak out. What's a' the hullaballoo?' demanded Miss Janet, her imperious curiosity, together with her clear conscience, getting the better of her late decorous politeness.

Thus adjured, Miss Bethia did not know how to refuse replying. Besides, she, too, was destitute of any serious apprehension, and regarded the affair—which no doubt had given her a little fright, in spite of its absurdity—as a foolish mistake.

'It's twa shirra-officers, I think, come in a cab, sayin' they have a warrant for us.'

'A warrant!' cried Eneas, horrified; 'an arrest for debt, you mean? I had no idea of this. Yes, I will speak to the men, of course,' he continued, in some agitation. 'But I must see you out first, Miss Drysdale. This—this misfortune, of which I had no conception, is not a thing for you to be mixed up with.'

'Don't mind me, Mr. Mackinnon,' said Clary, still mistress of herself, though she looked startled. 'I shall go in a minute, if you wish it; but can I be of no use? My father is not in town, but my brother is at the office. Could he do nothing?'

'Debt!' shrieked Miss Janet, who had been struck dumb by the unfounded accusation. 'We do not owe a sillar saxpence. We never did, when we were near starvation—ladies though we were: that you did not ken of, Eneas, you that have evened us to debt!'

'I have no wish to intrude,' the civil enough, but grave-sounding voice of the constable spoke from the hall. The speaker followed the voice with his person, punctiliously removing his hat as he entered the room, but making good his entrance. 'I must come in to do my duty. I had better explain this is not an arrest for debt; it is a warrant from the fiscal to take the three auld leddies before a magistrate.'

The outrage was so inconceivable that Miss Janet laughed aloud, while Miss Bethia's vague terror returned, and Miss Mackinnon appealed helplessly:

'Wha is he? The drummer? But whaur's his drum? Did we lose onything yesterday, Janet—Betheye?'

'What on earth is the pretence for this extraordinary proceeding? There must be some huge blunder,' insisted Eneas. 'These are my aunts—the Miss Mackinnons—who have lived here for more than half a century. They are well known in Glasgow—hundreds will speak to their respectability. Good heavens! who has doubted it?'

'I have nothing to say against it, sir,' answered the inflexible servant of the law. 'I presumed these were the Miss Mackinnons, and I have a warrant to take them up.'

'On what charge?'

'The charge I am ready to tell you. It is the wilful and malicious burning of the will of the late Archibald Fenton of Strathdivie, at Strathdivie, on the 11th of this month, by May Mackinnon, Janet Mackinnon, and Elizabeth or Bethia Mackinnon. I have to caution the prisoners against saying anything.'

'The thing is preposterous,' protested the Lieutenant. 'It is true my aunts have just returned from Strathdivie, where they went for the funeral of their relative, but you may as well accuse them of setting fire to his house as of burning his will. What do you say, Aunt Janet?' asked Eneas almost cheerfully, his confidence re-established by the incredibility of the charge.

'That we brunt it, sure enough, and what for no?' demanded the undaunted woman. 'The wull had no concern with onybody save oursel's, unless it were a couple of servants. Archie Fenton had got out his spite at me and Meye by making an eldest dochter—or, as some say, an eldest son—of Betheye, who would not lend hersel' to sic treachery, so we agreed among oursel's to turn the tables upon the man by burning the wull and dividing the money fair. We'll see that the servants have their legacy, which is mair than ane of them deserves—an impident hizzie—but that's neither here nor there. Now what have you to say against it, Lieutenant? There's no fraud or wrang done; it was to prevent wrang; neither law nor gospel can object to that. I cannot tell what the man means. I suppose the writer body was angered at not getting a job. But I've explained,' ended Miss Janet, in perfect assurance that her explanation was satisfactory.

Miss Mackinnon and Miss Betheye were equally convinced. Miss Betheye was again shaking off her alarm, and feeling some amount of complacency for the part she had played in the matter.

'I would not have touched a farthing of

what should have been Meye's and Janet's,' she added her version of the story; 'and as long as the wull was there, they wouldna tak' their ain from me, at my pleasure, and me the youngest. There was nothing for it but to destroy the paper, which had only to do with our business, and mak' a new settlement.'

As for Miss Mackinnon, she darted her hawk's glance all around, and actually chuckled.

Eneas Mackinnon stood the picture of despair.

'How could you be so mad?' he broke out, with passion that was strange in the man. 'I thought even old women had more sense.'

Claribel Drysdale touched him on the arm, and drew him a little aside.

'Don't you see, your aunts meant no harm,' she whispered; 'it was an accident. Don't undeceive them yet. It would be barbarous. I'll go with them to the magistrate.'

'Impossible!' he exclaimed. 'What would your father think? You are an angel of goodness, but——'

'No, no,' she said, with a faint smile; 'I am not very good. I am only an idle girl up in town for a day, and I have nothing particular to do when nearly all my friends are away.'

'But your father——'

'My father has the greatest respect for your aunts as worthy representatives of one of the old Glasgow families. He would be glad that I should do anything for them in an awkward dilemma.'

'I know I ought not to allow it,' he began to hesitate; 'it would be very unpleasant for you; and where would be the use?'

'The magistrate may be an acquaintance of mine, or he may know my name—my father has some influence. Go for my brother, and try what he can do. You must not seek to prevent me from accompanying the Miss Mackinnons, if the men will let me, and I think we can manage that. There is no other woman to go with them, and they may break down when they learn the truth.'

Eneas stood and looked at Claribel like a man struck dumb and fascinated. He had always guessed that she was wise and capable, but he had never known what she could do when there was a call for the exercise of her powers. He obeyed her— nay, Miss Janet obeyed her, after she had cried out violently that the magistrate might come to her—she would not stir a foot to go to him. Let them put a finger on her if they daured. The Lieutenant would take care of that, though he had to send for his swurd to strike a blow for his aunties, and for social order in their persons.

'But we are all going, Miss Janet,' said Claribel calmly. 'All we ladies are going. You will not refuse to accompany your sisters and me.'

'Weel, if you are proposin' to mak' a ploy o't,' yielded Miss Janet doubtfully, 'if you want to tak' a ride through the streets to see the toon—only you can do that ony day from your mammaw's carriage.'

'But I have not you or the other Miss Mackinnons to bear me company,' said Clary promptly.

'Nor Eneas here,' said Miss Janet, falling into the trap. 'There will be room for him on the dickie.'

'No,' said Claribel, with the same clear decision that was apt to carry everything before it at home and abroad. 'He is going for my brother, to help to put an end to this little difficulty; but they will join us immediately.'

By sheer force of character, and by taking the lead—a proceeding unlooked for and extraordinary where her age and sex were concerned, but warrantable when there was no one else to stand in the breach—since the man entitled to act was stupefied and sick to the bottom of his soul with affront and dismay—Clary grasped the situation, controlled the other actors in it, and did the best that could be done under the circumstances. She gave Eneas a hint of what he was to try to do in another brief aside.

'You know, Mr. Mackinnon'—she allowed him credit for knowledge which had not yet come to him—'your aunts must not be detained a moment longer than can be helped. Somebody must find bail for them. Oh! it will be very easy—my father, if he could be got in time, Dr. Peter Murray—oh! dozens of people will be willing.'

He departed instantly to fulfil her behests. He had not her quick, practical brain, her unfaltering self-reliance, her moral courage; but he had, at least, the merit of appreciating them when he found them. He was ready to worship her, to make her his guiding star, to be twice the man with her that he would have been without her.

All Glasgow rang with the news when it was noised abroad that the Miss Mackinnons, of St. Mungo's Square, had been taken before a magistrate on a charge of felony. Some laughter, but far more horror and pity, were called forth. As Claribel Drysdale had said, dozens of citizens were willing to be bail for the unfortunate ladies. They were not detained more than an hour, during which Miss Janet was so smoothed down and held in check by Clary's peculiar tact and firmness, that the chief offender refrained from adding to her foolish vindication of her heinous misdemeanour the fresh offence of gratuitously insulting the magistrate.

The Miss Mackinnons were at home again without having incurred much harm. The misfortune was that the business could not rest there. The case, on the face of it, must be sent for trial. No exercise of interest on the ladies' behalf could prevent the necessity for them to take their places where other offenders had stood before them, in the public court, and run the risk of a sentence which, to old women, born and bred as they had been, was all but synonymous with death. Tam Drysdale was at his wits' end, and with many another kindly Glasgow man, full of Glasgow spirit, was willing to spare neither time, trouble, nor expense to help his townswomen in the strait into which their ignorance and rashness had brought them. The best counsel would be got, every available witness procured, and every extenuating circumstance receive a full hearing, as if the old Virginian Mackinnon were still making Glasgow 'trim'le' at the wag of his finger.

Tam made no objection to Claribel's remaining in town, and going often to St. Mungo's Square. He was proud to think that one of his daughters had shown such presence of mind, and been able to prove her loyalty to ladies in adversity. If it was any comfort to them for Clary to call on them, to do what she could to cheer and counsel them, they were heartily welcome to the comfort, so far as he and mother were concerned. Clary was only a girl, but the Miss Mackinnons might listen to less sensible encouragement and advice, though he said it who, perhaps, should not say it.

For any delicate reason why Claribel ought not to be conspicuously mixed up with the Mackinnons and their affairs, auld Tam could dismiss it without another consideration. He was entirely of opinion that this calamity to the whole Mackinnon family would knock on the head the wildest pretensions of the 'offisher lad' to Clary's favour. He could never be so base—Tam had almost said—even if she would listen to him, as to propose to connect himself with the Drysdales, after the fellow's aunts had rubbed shoulders with the hulks, and after what he—Tam Drysdale—was striving to do to avert the catastrophe. The thing was clean out of the question.

Stout-hearted as Miss Janet was, the trial hanging over her, with the restlessness of Miss Mackinnon, the lamentations of Miss Bethia, the stern remonstrances and injunctions of the lawyers, broke her down, comparatively. While she still stuck to the point that she and her sisters had meant no ill and were morally entitled to pursue the course they had adopted, she ceased to indulge in hectoring. Nay, on the great day when she had to face judge, jury, and crowded court, she was brought to the extreme length of not speaking till she was spoken to. And when Miss Janet was tamed, all were tamed, though Miss Mackinnon struggled painfully with her infirmity, and Miss Bethia looked well-nigh distracted.

Claribel Drysdale was present, but she did not sit near the old ladies. That place was for their agitated, handsome nephew from the Barracks. But it was she who had suggested to him to take it, and it was she who had induced Lady Semple to come with Dick and express her sympathy with her son's friend. Moreover, Claribel admitted that she was in the Court at once to maintain the spirits of her singular charge, and to do what she could to keep them in order.

The judges were in their seats. The jury were sworn in. The Miss Mackinnons had surrendered to their friends' bail, and pled guilty; the case was argued in earnest on both sides. It was no mere form or piece of mockery for as simple and ridiculous a transgression as ever the law laid hold of. On the one hand were ranged the insubordination of the proceeding, the aggravation of its committal by persons of birth, education, and mature years, its evil as a precedent. On the other hand were marshalled the absence of criminal intent on the part of the offenders, their stupid but honest ignorance of the law, their frank and full admission of what they had done the moment the question was put to them, with the crowning extenuation that they had not devised wrong to any human being by their lawless act; they had merely agreed among themselves to divide, as they judged, more fairly the money which had come to them by right.

The law might say that this was a lame defence, but what right-minded man could refuse to admit its cogency?

All unseemly demonstrations of curiosity and amusement were put down while the verdict was in suspense. As a matter of fact there could only be one—that of guilty —to which indeed the Miss Mackinnons had pled. The question was, what would be the relative mildness or severity of the sentence the judge must deliver? The trespass against authority had been as audacious as trespass could be; but in consideration of the freedom from malice, and the sex and age of the trespassers, justice was tempered with mercy.

One month's imprisonment, without hard labour, in Glasgow Gaol, was awarded to the three Miss Mackinnons.

'My lord——' said Miss Janet, recovering from her dumbness and stumbling to her feet. But she was denied a last protest. She and her sisters were surrounded and hurried out of Court.

CHAPTER XXIX.

'LOVE WILL VENTURE IN WHERE WISDOM AINCE HAS BEEN.'

CLARY was the first to utter a modified congratulation. The result might have been so much worse.

'Never mind, Miss Janet; a month will soon be over. Everybody knows you meant no harm. It was all that horrid Fenton of Strathdivie, with his ridiculous will. Your friends will come and see you on all the visiting-days.'

'Lassie,' said Miss Janet, for she had grown familiar with her young ally, 'do you think I would demean mysel' to mak' a moan, though we've been waur tret than thieves and vagabonds—hiz that have paid our taxes, the police-tax among them—every shillin' to the Queen and country, since the year that my father died? I was only going to tell the judge that there had been word of our great-grandfather being sent to the Tooer of London, for although he was not just out with Prince Charlie, there was no doubt that the Mackinnon of that day waited on the Prince at Shawfield House. It would better have become the Croon to give his descendants lodgings in the Tooer, if so be we were to suffer imprisonment for settin' wrang richt, than to send us to the common jile.'

'Oh, Janet,' Miss Bethia wailed, 'think of the journey for Meye! They may put irons on us in the jile, but they cannot bring us to the block there.'

'The block!' cried Miss Janet. 'It would be the hangman's wuddie [gallows].'

'No, no,' Clary interposed fearlessly. 'Why do you frighten your sister, Miss Janet, and slander the powers that be? You will only have to stay in comfortable rooms where you can have books and work and anything you wish, till you come out and return to your own house in St. Mungo's Square, in the course of four weeks.'

When the Miss Mackinnons had tasted the penalties of modern captivity, had survived the first shock, and found themselves not fatally injured by it, they were heard to say that prisoners did not know what it was to live. If they had learnt to deny themselves, and to fare as ladies and gentlemen had often to fare, they would think little of imprisonment—rather, they would count it, if they had done no wrong of which they ought to repent and be ashamed, a very decent sort of refuge! Certainly folk could not get out when they wanted, but then they did not want to go out in rainy weather —and when did it not rain in the west? There was never a loss without a compensation. As for anything else—bed and board, fuel and light, the sufferers by the law's severity were bold to complain. It was the innocent people that had to keep up comfortable gaols who were entitled to cry out, and perhaps it was but just that some time or other they should reap the benefit of what they had long contributed to maintain.

Unquestionably the Miss Mackinnons, in the philosophic spirit at which they had arrived, had all the alleviations which could be procured for them in their peculiar circumstances. Among these were the constant visits of Claribel Drysdale, who never missed a visiting-day. She had taken the Miss Mackinnons regularly under her protection. How and why she endured what was so antagonistic to her own taste, nobody could tell. The fact remained that she did it. She knew, as Maggie Craig had known before her, that the eccentric old ladies were come of the cream of old Glasgow; that in reality, some of their objectionable qualities were the growth of the arrogance and irreproachability of their ancient social claims. But then Claribel Drysdale had cared nothing for any cream of Glasgow, old or new; she had appeared to build her hopes and ambitions on a different foundation. Was it that, having been drawn into the use of her finer faculties, she enjoyed the exercise too keenly to be willing to relinquish it, or to consent to forego its reward? Was it that the rage of conquest came over her, conquest of elements the most opposed to those in her own character, conquest of herself as well as of others; a proud determination to show that she was equal to any difficulty, and mistress of it before she had done? Was it simply that deep down in Claribel Drysdale's calm, strong, well-balanced nature, there was a fountain of self-devotion, and one had unlocked the spring? He possessed other and more evident attractions for her; but was the most potent attraction of all really what was helpless and hopeless in him, which, in place of provoking and repelling her, appealed irresistibly to her strength of purpose, her instinct of ruling, and talent for making the best of things?

Among Clary's tastes had not been the rustic one of early rising, which had been found in her sister Eppie. Yet Claribel was, at this time, repeatedly the first at the breakfast-table at Drysdale Hall, which, as in all similar establishments, was regulated with a view to the men of the house setting off for business before the idler world was stirring. Clary would make the most unfaltering request for the use of the carriage at an unheard-of hour in the morning. Neither did she make the smallest concealment of her object. She was going to drive in to Glasgow, to the City prison, to see the Miss Mackinnons. She wished to be there as soon as the gates were opened.

Eppie junior marvelled; young Tam stared; Eppie senior looked troubled, but shrank from interfering. Auld Tam was blind. He even glanced up from his ham and egg to express his approbation.

'It's very gude of you, Clary, to think of the auld leddies in the trouble, in which there is no disgrace—none to forbid your going among them, even without your mither, at this hour. Still, it is very mindful and pretty of you, my dear.'

'Not at all,' said Claribel, turning her handsome face, unmoved in its clear paleness, on her father; 'I go to please myself. I have taken the Miss Mackinnons under my care. They are my old ladies now.'

Plenty of people were remarking significantly on Miss Drysdale's extraordinary attentions to three old, unattractive women, the victims of their idiotic conceit and silliness. Mrs. Drysdale well knew this, though she could not bring herself to transfer the knowledge to a quarter from which it might be energetically acted upon. Ill-natured tongues even went so far as to say that Lady Semple was enough a woman of the world to keep herself out of the entanglement. She had shown a little kindliness on her own account to the Miss Mackinnons because they had really become objects of pity, and her son had been in the same regiment and on intimate terms with young Mackinnon. But she had taken care never to accompany Claribel Drysdale to the gaol—Claribel Drysdale, who had been so particular and had not thought any man in Glasgow fit for her! She must have been engaged beforehand to the nephew—a penniless officer. Why had auld Tam Drysdale permitted it? Why did he not interfere now and put a stop to the engagement, when it was almost certain that Mr. Mackinnon must leave the army, and no longer retain his claim to as much as a subaltern's rank and a starvation income? A fine end to Claribel Drysdale's proud pretensions!

But auld Tam was possessed by another idea, and saw nothing of what was passing before his very eyes.

The last time Clary drove, before women like her were to be seen abroad, to that strange destination for a girl in the upper classes, and waited in the carriage till the time to enter, she caught a glimpse of Eneas

Mackinnon, with a similar intention, standing where he could best escape observation. Even from the little she could see of him, she could judge that he looked ill and dejected. The next moment she alighted and walked towards him, coming up behind him and making him turn, startled by the quiet mention of his name—' Mr. Mackinnon.'

He shook hands with her in silence, colouring highly as he did so.

' Why don't you say " well met "?' she rallied him.

' Well met here !' he exclaimed with more desperate sadness than bitterness, for he was hardly ever a bitter man.

' Yes; why not here, when it is for the last time? Your aunts will be free in three days.'

' Well, I suppose for their sakes I ought to rejoice,' he said with an effort; ' as I should thank you for your great kindness to them.'

' No, indeed; no thanks. I told my father

that already this morning. I come to please myself. I have taken the old ladies under my wing.'

He looked at her wistfully, but when he spoke again he had dropped her out of the conversation.

'I ought not to grudge them their release, poor old souls,' he said slowly. 'They brought me up, and have always cared for me a hundred times more than I deserve, and I have not been able to do anything for them. I know now, though I was a dolt at the time, that when my aunt Bethia had fever, the whole family might have died of starvation, but for the help which your father and Dr. Murray gave them. I may well forgive the most egregious of their blunders—of course they did not know the mischief they were doing to themselves or any other person. But they have put the finishing-touch to my disadvantages—to the gross mistake which stranded me in the army—not that I have any reason to suppose I could have done much good in any other profession. I had better walk into the Clyde at once, and save myself and my friends further trouble which will be ill repaid.'

'You—a soldier!' she said, in her low distinct voice.

'I shall not be a soldier much longer,' he declared. 'Why should I bring a slur upon the service to which I have been a small gain at the best, by continuing in it after the pass to which my people have brought themselves and me?' and he looked up at the prison walls. 'This is a little incident in my family history which will not be forgotten.'

'Don't seek that it should be forgotten—a foolish, I grant you very foolish, but perfectly guileless mistake of three old ladies—why, it was a thing innocent children might have done. I wish your brother officers may have nothing worse to reveal in the histories of their families,' she said fearlessly.

'You are too good,' he told her again.

'But the very absurdity of the affair will perpetuate its memory. I do not wish to blame anybody, I do not wish to crave pity from you; but it is the last straw which breaks the camel's back.'

'Then the camel should get somebody else to help to bear it.'

'Who would?' he asked quickly. 'I have nothing to offer in return but the miserable pittance of a lieutenant in a marching regiment, which I can only make pay my own expenses by scraping and saving. Miss Drysdale, you can't tell what a manager I am,' he said, with a little bitterness this time; 'how I save up my stores and make my old clothes do double duty, like an old woman. What would the rich young Glasgow fellows think if they saw behind the scenes? They have a tolerably accurate knowledge, indeed, that I am impecunious, but wouldn't they laugh awfully at my dodges?'

'The rich young Glasgow fellows,' she said, with scorn, 'would half empty their purses to be like you in some respects, and they would do well to make the little sacrifice. But I know more of the rich young Glasgow girls. I suppose you would say we were very extravagant; at least, so Lady Semple tells me. We would give more for a lace flounce, or a fur trimming, than would keep a poor, respectable middle-class family for a year. And it is not all in bad taste, some of us dress tolerably well—confess it, Mr. Mackinnon,' she demanded—gaily for Clary, who was generally too dignified to be gay.

'Your dress, like everything else about you, is perfection; and that's what drives poor devils to destruction,' he muttered, half piqued, half-puzzled.

'I have always liked to dress well, and to dress in a way that becomes a rich man's daughter; but do you suppose I should care to do it if—if I were a poor man's wife? Don't you see it would no longer be in keeping? It is not so much the dress as the sense of fitness I mind.'

'But you would not be in your right place as a poor man's wife,' he said in agitation; 'no penniless wretch of a subaltern would presume.'

'We were not talking of subalterns,' she said demurely; 'and as for presumption, could it be presumption if the person most concerned did not think so?'

'Claribel!' he said.

'Eneas!' she answered.

'It would be dishonourable in me to take advantage of your generosity.' He struggled to act up to his conception of the character of a gentleman. 'I can hardly keep myself—we should have to be dependent on your father. He would never consent. I have felt before now that he desired to hold me at arm's length—that you might have nothing to say to me, though lately he has not thought it worth his while to use such precautions. He has been a good friend to my poor old aunts in their trouble; but I have sunk fathoms in his estimation, socially.'

She listened without contradicting him; indeed, she admitted candidly:

'I don't say you are wrong. My father has a greater respect for the old than for the young Mackinnons. He does not think you are a match for a Drysdale.' It was plain speaking, and he winced. She went on—'But when I marry, it will be I who marry, and not my father. No one knows that better than he, and he is good and kind, as well as clever and successful. He is respected for more than his wealth and social position. I am sure he could not be utterly inconsistent if he tried.'

'I have no doubt your father is all you say,' said the Lieutenant, but in anything rather than an assured tone.

'He's not a small tyrant,' insisted Claribel. 'He is neither unfair nor cruel. He may disapprove, but he will not long dispute my right of choice, or refuse me a daughter's portion, when he is convinced that I am in earnest.'

'I trust you are right,' he said nervously;

'but it seems too splendidly good news to be true; I cannot believe it. I fear I must be taking a mean advantage of your——'

'Simplicity,' she finished his sentence for him with a laugh. 'No, don't treat me as a simpleton, and please don't distress yourself on my account, as if I had become your prey—for it is really too good of you. I have always known what I was about—always seen and taken what suited me best; and if I find, on mature consideration, that you suit me—why need you object? You don't really, else I should not have said what I have—I should not be here at all, I dare say.'

'Object!' he exclaimed, in a tone which carried conviction with it.

'There is one advantage of being come of the people,' she proceeded calmly. 'Have you never observed how much the rich Glasgow girls manage their own lives and settle their fortunes? I am not a great admirer of the causes which have led to such a result, but I have always claimed my independence, and prized it, and my father would be the last to seek to deprive me of it.'

'I hope you are right,' he said emphatically.

'I am right,' she told him; 'neither my father nor my mother are, even in theory, aristocratic parents. They would never dream of coercing their children—at least, not their daughters. I am not certain whether my father might not have been tempted to use indirect influence where my brother was concerned, to get him to enter the business, my father's heart was so set upon it. But that is quite another thing from interfering with his daughters in what is their affair. If my father is not altogether willing, I don't think your aunts will find fault,' she said, with a womanly archness that was both wonderful and charming in Clary.

'No, indeed; but how shall I ever thank you?'

'By believing and trusting me. Don't

you see that will be your duty and privilege henceforth?'

Thus, in the raw morning, in that doleful place, where miserable men and women were wont to meet and part, two hearts went together and sang their song of joy, as if they had been in Eden. At the gate of Glasgow Gaol, Claribel Drysdale, the proudest girl in Glasgow, plighted her troth and resigned her liberty—if that could be called resigning, which was in fact taking Eneas Mackinnon under her protection, and determining to make the most of him, as of herself, in all time to come.

CHAPTER XXX.

A HORRIBLE SUSPICION ASSAILS AULD TAM.

WHAT was auld Tam about, that he could permit his eldest daughter, his 'edicate, handsome, tochered lass,' to throw herself away on a cool beggar of a penniless soldier—a man without the brains to keep his old relations from a deed which had landed them in Glasgow Gaol, and awakened the mingled laughter and pity of the whole city, the whole country? The very monstrousness of such a conjecture, the very audacity of Eneas Mackinnon's continuing to have hopes and claims, served to put Tam off his guard. He never dreamt that any precautions were necessary after the Miss Mackinnons had done for themselves and their grand-nephew effectually.

There was more than magnanimity and good feeling in Tam's exertions on the old ladies' behalf—there was a certain serious conviction that in making them, all danger from that quarter was over. And auld Tam would have been right if he had not left Clary out of his calculations—if he had not failed to make allowance for a tenacity of purpose and power of getting her own way by bending everything and everybody, including the chief obstacles to her will, and the very persons who ought to have had the deciding vote, to do her bidding.

With Clary to overrule circumstances and constrain Eneas Mackinnon to follow her lead, Tam ought never to have been sure of what might or might not happen. But in addition to his false security in the persuasion that the 'offisher lad' would not have the face any longer to look at Clary, and that the girl herself had listened to reason and was actuated by motives of mere philanthropy, Tam Drysdale's attention was suddenly violently distracted and held fast in another direction. A crowd of interests of greater importance—nay, of vital moment—pressed upon him, till the question of Clary and her settlement in life dwindled into a drop in the bucket, a speck on the horizon.

On the very day that Claribel's future was settled at the gaol-door, her father had gone to the office of a solicitor named Greig, who had been employed in the Miss Mackinnons' case, whose bill auld Tam had taken it upon him to discharge. The bill was not longer than he had expected, and he was not the man to grudge it, so that he was in a placid enough frame of mind. Having come a little distance, he felt inclined to tarry a moment and talk at his ease, particularly as the owner of the office was an exceptionally pleasant old gentleman, possessed of a good deal of curious professional information, beyond what was of a private and confidential nature, which he had no objection to air for the benefit of his clients.

'As I told you, Mr. Drysdale,' said Mr. Greig—a stout, bald-headed man who sat facing his visitor, slightly flourishing a pencil and laying down the law, which was in a manner his own property—'the ladies may be thankful they got off as they did. It is an old story, the contract which gave them a claim on Strathdivie. I'm not quite clear that Fenton might not have disputed it; you see, there was a certain power vested in the Fentons, which was in itself something of a flaw. But marriage contracts are, like the marriages they represent, not things to parry with. They are about as bad as trusteeships; and I consider that it must be a most extraordinary will which gives more trouble and brings more grist to the lawyer's mill, than these two other devices of the enemy.'

'Do you say so, sir?' answered Tam, who did not at the moment care much about the statement, but who had a shrewd, intelligent man's general desire to receive trustworthy information on any subject, not to say on one which cropped up periodically in most family histories. 'I had no marriage contract, for the very good reason that I had little enough to settle on my wife when I got her. But after a man has made some money, and has dochters belonging to him, it may be as well for him to ken what is necessary on the subject. Now that I come to think of it, I have a marriage settlement which came accidentally into my possession not very long syne.' Some feeling of delicacy and not of craftiness prevented auld Tam from saying whose marriage settlement it was. He only added, after an instant, while the lawyer listened as if he were on the alert for what might concern himself, 'I had almost forgotten the existence of the paper, in place of putting it into the hands of the person who has most richt to it.'

'Then this is a most fortuitous conversation,' said Mr. Greig briskly. 'Take my advice, sir, and do not let the grass grow on your forwarding the deed to its proper destination. You are not aware what weighty issues may hang on its contents.'

'Houts, Mr. Greig!' exclaimed Tam, a little impatiently. 'It has not to do with any living creature. Both of the contracting parties are dead, after having cleverly disposed of what they contracted for, mair than twenty years syne.'

'That does not matter a brass farthing,' insisted Mr. Greig, as if he enjoyed the irrelevancy of the protest, and the superiority of marriage contracts to such trifles as death and the making away with worldly goods. 'Marriage contracts have to do with generations unborn, whom they fetter beforehand. They are no joke, Mr. Drysdale. Why, the very settlement that led indirectly to the act of which the Miss Mackinnons were guilty, might have opened your eyes alike to the security and the danger of marriage contracts.'

Tam was startled; but he failed as yet to see what might be the full significance of the communication to him.

'I understand about a charge like that on the estate of Strathdivie,' he said deliberately; 'but you do not mean to say that a dead man, by the stroke of a pen, could control sale and purchase, and hinder the business of the world where his bairns' bairns, or heirs farther off still, were in question? Let us suppose a case,' he continued, warming to the dispute, and feeling a thrill, as it were, of premonition pass through him when he gave with double consciousness his imaginary example. 'A bargain has been made without heed to an existing marriage contract, maybe without the knowledge of sic a trap, though, according to your tale, it is binding on both the bargainers; do you mean to tell me that the paction will be broken and some innocent man condemned to loss, because he had the misfortune to be ignorant of what was out of his way? What justice would there be in that?'

'I'm not prepared to say about the justice,' said Mr. Greig cautiously. 'There may be two sides to the question, and a good deal of argument on either side. But I can speak for the law—*that* goes as far as you say.'

'Then I take leave to say I'll have a poorer opinion of the law from this day,' said Tam stiffly. 'I was wont to think that law and justice in this country were as nearly ane as human frailty would alloo; but, if I'm to trust a legal authority, I've been in error.'

'I beg your pardon, my dear sir; there are limits to marriage contracts,' said Mr. Greig, stroking his own bald head softly. He did not wish to offend an influential client, neither did he like—to his credit— to wound an honest man.

'I should hope so,' said Tam sharply.

'We have been speaking vaguely,' went on the other, with increasing suavity; 'we have been implying, for one thing, that there are descendants to profit by the contract, which, by-the-bye, is registered and placed where all men may read it, if they will.'

'Humph!' said Tam, 'and what if they are not readers of sic documents? What if they never heard tell of sic a privilege or needcessity—whichever you may like to call it.'

Mr. Greig began again to smooth down the crown of his head tenderly, as if it had been the man he was addressing.

'You've had enough to do with heritable property, Mr. Drysdale, to be well acquainted with the nature of title-deeds. You know that every prudent man—I may say, every man in his sober senses—will desire to see such deeds before he invests in the lands or the houses that the papers represent. Well then, marriage contracts are not so far out of the category. A purchaser who has any reason to suppose there may have been such a contract, or indeed without supposing at all, for the greater assurance of himself and his family, is bound to apply for a warrant, called "a search," to satisfy himself that there is no prior obligation to interfere with his future rights.'

'That is to say,' said Tam, with a fine flavour of irony, 'he should prepare for falling among thieves.'

'He might do worse,' said the lawyer, with a laugh, declining to make a personal application of the remark. 'I am aware that the precaution is often neglected among acquaintances and friends, but it ought not to be. You know the Spanish proverb, about not trusting your own father to count money.'

'It is a blackguard saying!' cried Tam indignantly.

'I am afraid it is,' admitted Mr. Greig candidly. 'But apart from that, there may be ignorance, as you said, on both sides, in selling without the liberty to sell, as well as in buying without the power to buy. Surely, without any prejudice, it is a duty to guard against the possibility of such mutually ruinous ignorance, though there are other laws that offer some compensation to the unwary.'

'I cannot stop to hear them; and I am

free to own that what I have heard does not recommend itself to me. But marriage contracts are not things that I have ony troke with as yet,' he added with sudden decision while he rose, 'even if I had not got enough of law for one day—if you will forgive me for saying so, Mr. Greig,' ended Tam, recovering his natural courtesy.

Mr. Greig balanced his pencil between his fingers after Tam had left him, and pondered a moment.

'I thought auld Tam Drysdale had been less stupid and better informed,' he ruminated, with a shade of professional narrowness. 'He is more intolerant and less reasonable than I had pictured him. I dare say his success is wasting him and making a bully of him—I have often seen the process—or he may have been bitten in some of his purchases; they say he is adding field to field, and buying in all the small crofts about Drysdale Haugh. These prosperous men hate to be beaten in the value of a halfpenny. Anyway, he will not grant even to himself that he has come off the loser by the business. He's a dour dog, auld Tam, but he's not the worst sort. I was a fool to stroke him the wrong way; however, he's not the kind that bears malice.'

The lawyer—lawyer though he was—failed to connect the momentary heat which Tam had shown, with his voluntary announcement, at the beginning of the conversation, that he had come into the possession of a marriage contract which was none of his. Nor, for that matter, did Tam in so many words acknowledge to himself that there was any link between the two facts, unless by the vehemence with which he kept repeating, as he drove out the same afternoon to Drysdale Hall, that he had nothing to do with such riddles, such provisions made, and snares laid for the unsuspecting.

Mrs. Gavin Mackinnon, Miss Craig that was, had given her husband the power of selling Drysdale Haugh and the dyeworks to Tam Drysdale. Why should she have been at the trouble and expense of granting the man such power, if it was not hers to grant, if in professing to do so she defrauded generations unborn—generations descended from her and Guy Mackinnon? Would she not take care that everything was plain when it was so much her own interest to be careful? He, Tam Drysdale, had bought the place in good faith, with honest money, hardly won, and the farm and the works had belonged to his father's kinsman—to a Drysdale, long before the name of Mackinnon had been heard on the Aytoun Water. Who would be mad enough to dispute Tam's purchase? What law was there in the universe that could dare to call itself law, and at the same time question his title to Drysdale Haugh?

But was there any mention of heirs in that ill-preserved, ill-gotten contract between Eneas Mackinnon and Margaret Craig which had reached him—Tam Drysdale—by a strange mischance, if not by a projected fraud?

He could not for the life of him answer the question, at which he kept quarrying afresh during every mile of the road between Glasgow and Drysdale Hall. Was there no mention of children in the contract, as there certainly was not in that will of old Drysdale's, for which Tam had proposed to barter the other? or was there no such coincidence, which would in itself, perhaps, have been singular? Had he merely overlooked the clause because the paper had struck him as worse than useless, a record of disappointed hopes and lost opportunities?

All the time that Tam was scouting the apprehension as unreasonable and impracticable, and telling himself what a fool he was to suffer even a momentary scare from the long-winded sentences and long-nebbed words of a book-man — a lawyer — he harassed himself with a fruitless effort to satisfy this doubt. 'Whitebreeks' went through his paces uselessly, where his master was concerned. For once the schoolchildren, lingering for him at Birlie Brae, looked wistfully in his face, and meeting no responsive glance, shrank from hanging on to the dogcart, and fell back discomfited, deprived of the ride which he himself had described as so sweet a pleasure to juvenile trespassers. Auld Tam neither saw their wonder and disappointment, nor did he observe beast or bird, field or hedgerow, on his homeward way through the stubble-fields, and between the hedges growing red with hips and haws. He was in a brown study—most unusual with him—the whole road.

Thompson, the groom, glancing askance at his master, gave his own head ever so slight a shake—either auld Tam was on the verge of a fit of apoplexy, or, as the idea of any other loss of power in that quarter was unfamiliar to the servant, he judged his master must have made another leap to the heights of fortune, which would land him among dukes and earls, and take him away from driving in a dogcart to and from a city office. But would he ever be so happy again in the highest places, as when Thompson drove him behind 'Whitebreeks' as regular as the clock, going over the ground—every inch of which he knew —in a given time, neither too fast nor too slow, but just what was fit for a gentleman of auld Tam's years and substance, with the progress made between his grand house and his place of business, where he had risen from being a working man and earned all his money? Thompson made the reflection on his own account sentimentally.

The spell was not broken by the appearance of the two Eppies, ready to meet and greet the husband and father. Yet neither did their presence, nor the sight of Drysdale Hall, in what its master had fondly regarded as its perfection, inflict a pang, as they might have done, or might come to do. He only saw them as in a dream. The most active trouble he was sensible of assailed him when his eye fell upon young Tam, whose hours were not the same as his father's, and who generally returned by the railway, which had a station near the bleachfield. His father had been so eager to embark young Tam with him in the business in which he was now a partner, with a share in its liabilities as well as its profits, that the elder man had forgotten the responsibilities which he laid upon his son.

Auld Tam put a force upon himself—he had early learnt self-mastery—he met the advances of his family, he went and dressed for dinner, and sat at the foot of his table in the ordinary fashion. But the impulse was strong upon him to dispense with the usual arrangements and burdensome formalities, including the eating of the principal meal of the day, set all aside, retire to his business-room, and there investigate the terror that—pretend to himself as he might—was chilling his blood and tugging every moment harder at his heart-strings.

Only love, watching auld Tam with Argus-eyes, detected that his appetite and his conversation were the result of a hard struggle. It was the elder Eppie who made the discovery, which astonished and even frightened her a little. But tender affection has its sure intuitions and is equal to most situations; besides, both of the Eppies had a fine good sense of their own. Mrs. Drysdale would not call attention to a mood of body and mind which it was clear her husband sought to keep to himself, by assailing him with observations and inquiries. She behaved with true delicacy—not even approaching him on the plea of ministering to his wants. She kept back young Eppie with her smaller experience, taking her aside and telling her simply father had 'a sore head,' and would prefer to be undisturbed; she might give him a song by-and-by, if he came into the drawing-room.

Supposing it was his heart and not his head which ailed auld Tam, Eppie, in the middle of her abounding sympathy, was willing to wait her husband's time to communicate his cares.

At last auld Tam could retreat to his den—his innocent stage for playing at being a laird and a J.P., where he had not even been cumbered by business routine. He closed the door, bolted it for the first time in his life, looked round on the engravings of reaping machines, Brobdignagian turnips and fat cattle, felt the discrepancy between the past and the present, and said grimly to himself, 'I micht be going to commit a murder,' and then went straight to his desk, unlocked it, and turned to the compartment in which he had put the two papers, till he could see Lieutenant Mackinnon about them. Succeeding events, conspicuous among them the danger in which the Miss Mackinnons had stood, had occupied him and prevented him from carrying out his intention. In fact, he had been hindered from thinking, with any distinct purpose, till that day of Sandy Macnab's call with Rory o' the Shelties, and of the deed and the contract which auld Tam had taken into his own hands, under the impression that the papers were safer with him than with a crazy Highland beggar. Certainly, when Tam had paid for them, it had been more from a movement of half-reluctant compassion for a miserable fatuous wretch who had deluded and overreached himself, than as offering a price for documents, one of which had no interest, and the other only a sentimental attraction, for him.

There were the two old battered but still perfectly legible papers, with the more modern slip appended by some officious pedantic Highland minister or schoolmaster, as Tam had left them, safe enough in truth. He began to wish he had never seen the deeds, that they had been relinquished to the tender mercies of a madman. If Sandy Macnab had not been so forward—if Rory had not been so greedy, and cunning, and weak of wit—if that strange minister or schoolmaster had not been so punctilious, the papers might have lain still where the careless, swaggering sinner Guy Mackinnon had left them, and plagued nobody.

But since they were here in his desk, by a queer coincidence, they must be dealt with.

Auld Tam sat down and proceeded to meet his fate. Yet, brave man as he was, he continued to dally with it, to tell himself he was grossly exaggerating the importance of the contents of one of these papers. Since Mrs. Mackinnon had given her husband the power to sell Drysdale Hall, such a power must have existed; neither he nor she could have been such an idiot as to take the power for granted, be guilty of an unlawful act, and commit a wrong against their children, born or unborn.

As it happened, the will which Tam Drysdale had looked at last, the only time he had gone over the deeds, was lying on the top of the contract. He took it up and began to read it through, word for word, as if it had been that with which he had to do—as if it were likely to contain some information which might throw light on the uncertainty with regard to the provisions of the other—an uncertainty which one glance at the proper place would determine for ever.

But old Drysdale's will disinheriting auld Tam's father had nothing more to say to his son than it had said before, even though he methodically reckoned up the period between the dates of the deaths of the uncle in Scotland and the adopted niece in India—which had made all the difference in the world in the succession, and enabled Maggie Craig to step into her mother's shoes and keep out the Drysdale cousin.

With one hard-drawn breath, auld Tam put down the will and took up the marriage contract, reading it as he had read the other, line by line and sentence by sentence, through a few of the ancient barbarous words and a dozen of the labyrinthian repetitions in which the law delights. At last he came to the technical phrases, standing out on the page as if to strike him a blow, written as if in letters of fire to burn into his brain the disastrous intimation which had decided between themselves that what was done could not be undone, and that the child would experience no great loss in the withdrawal from its keeping of a succession which had prospered so ill with his father and mother.

All had favoured the fatal blundering. Auld Tam was not free from blame. A dim recollection came back upon him which sickened him, as with a throe of remorse and rage, at his own infatuation. Somebody, he could no longer tell whom—some cautious old friend or sharp-sighted associate—had spoken to him of the possible existence of prior contracts, apart from the title-deeds, and advised a reference to them. And he had thought the friend timid, and the associate picking a hole in Tam's coat. For he, too, had been eager and set on his purchase. He had derided the idea of any obstacle. He had insisted that he knew all about Drysdale Haugh and the Mackinnons, and that in the face of such intimate acquaintance further trouble and expense were uncalled for. His penny-saving thrift, on which he had prided himself all his life, had come in and forbidden him to expend a few pounds in order to prevent the risk of thousands, the danger of a life's efforts and ambitions being frustrated at the eleventh hour.

CHAPTER XXXI.

THE SUSPICION BECOMES A CERTAINTY.

AULD TAM had not the right to a single one of the advantages on which he had prided himself. Nothing was his—neither lands nor works, neither old farmhouse nor modern mansion, nor office in Glasgow—at least, if any portion of what he had called his remained to him, the claim was so entangled, and so met and barred by other claims, that he could not unravel it.

The Mackinnons had sold, without a right, land and works. Tam had bought equally without a warrant. He would be entitled to his purchase-money back again, he supposed, if there was a grain of justice in men's laws; but that would be little in comparison to the rents and shares of profits he might be called on to refund, and the sums of money he had expended on buildings and improvements which he had made on another man's property without his consent, for which there was no reason that he should have compensation. If the miserable discovery had been made in other circumstances, there was just a chance that he might have surmounted it. He might have compounded for wrong done—without any evil intention on his part—in which as it had happened he had been the most cruelly wronged, and continued his business an impoverished but not a ruined man. It was otherwise this year, when, as he had known, he had need of not only all his available capital, but his unimpaired credit, to carry him through the pressure occasioned by extravagant outlay and over-trading, when there were dropping shots of failures on every side, like minute-guns at sea, gathering gloom on the Exchange, a glutted market, forced sales, short hours, improvident work-people beginning to starve without the apology of a strike, stinted indulgences, forbidden pleasures, haggard faces, heavy hearts, care and doubt, and dread for what was coming on all hands.

This was the reverse side of that splendid prosperity of which in its intoxication men had said, raving, that it would never come to an end; and Tam, who had seen both sides more than once before, had raved like the rest, with the least excuse, because he had boasted he had known all the turns of trade. He had been as blind and besotted as any tyro in commerce—blinder at the last than his own son Tam, who was new to the business. He had over-speculated and risked the most daring ventures, and he would have wanted all the help of a secure position and untrammelled reserves of power to bring the past year's undertakings to a successful issue—to prevent them, like Pharaoh's lean cattle, swallowing up their well-fleshed brethren—nay, so to control and compel them as to make them the instruments of the further building up of his fortunes, in spite of formidable odds, and of the extension and preservation of his name for deep sagacity and broadly-calculated enterprise.

Auld Tam had still hoped this with a high heart till his conversation with Mr. Greig in his office. What had been a faintly appalling suspicion then, was now a crushing reality; and he knew that to confess it publicly, as he was bound to do, and make restitution of what he had unawares acquired without the title to do so, meant simply, under present circumstances, dire ruin, without the hope of retrieving his losses. He could hardly even escape moral blame. Men might indeed free him from having been knowingly a party to the illegal transfer of Drysdale Haugh, which had rebounded so heavily on his own head; but they would not fail to accuse him of overconfidence and carelessness, and as 'give a dog a bad name and hang him,' so they would count as little less than criminal the magnitude of those far-afield speculations which had, as it proved, been raised on a foundation of sand, and not of rock. It would not matter—for the world never stopped to make such reservations—that he had been as ignorant of the instability of his foundation when he incurred these obligations, as the humblest bleacher or printer in his employment. Men would look at the whole story as giving the lie to the testimony by which they had united in calling him a prince and a ruler in trade, and had learned to put unbounded faith in his probity, his judgment, his discretion.

Tam Drysdale would be ruined without remedy, and he would ruin many another in his fall—from large firms, linked inseparably with his, to small contractors who had been his early comrades, like Willie Coates.

Auld Tam grew dizzy as he contemplated the catastrophe, and tried to take in all the consequences. Then he said he would sleep upon it, since it was a thing that no man could take action upon at a moment's notice. He replaced the papers in his desk, dropping them as if the fingers which could no longer retain them were palsied, locked them up, unfastened his room door, and walked out, feeling for the first time in his life that he had been up too early, had been in Glasgow at work all day, and was not so young as he had been. He said as much when he joined his family in the drawing-room; and his Eppie, glancing up quickly in his face, noticed, with a sharp pain, that her Tam looked ten years older since morning. His comely, fresh-coloured face was grey and lined, his eyes seemed sunken, the very carriage of his head was altered. Could it be the beginning of a sudden 'breaking-up' of his manly frame? She had heard of such unexpected, untimely breakings-up, specially in men of active habits, who had done as great things for themselves and their families as Tam Drysdale had done. It would break her heart for his sake; but if he were to become prematurely aged and infirm, if waiting upon him on her 'bended knees,' if nursing him every hour of the twenty-four, if studying every sick man's idle peevish fancy could solace him, he should have the solace—she would do it for her goodman, the lover of her youth, the father of her bairns, with her last breath, and it would be the greatest comfort left to her.

After auld Tam's admission of fatigue, it was natural that he should sit and rest in his chair, while young Eppie sang softly to him. Her mother wished she had not chosen 'The Land o' the Leal' for her first song; indeed, Tam himself interposed as if he could not bear it, saying,

'Not that, bairn; can you not give us something less dowie [sad] ?'

But when Eppie gave him 'Tak' your auld cloak about you,' he failed to beat time to the tune.

Tam supped composedly, to all outward appearance, but privately he felt as if he were swallowing, not to say borrowed, but stolen food, every morsel of which threatened to choke him. He lay awake during the long night, hearing every hour strike on the numerous clocks and timepieces which were no longer his any more than the bed he was stretched upon. It had been a whim of his to furnish every room with a timepiece, and to make it his business to see that the time in each case was told accurately. Now, every clock of them all combined to say that his days at Drysdale Hall were numbered, that still briefer was the space before he must tell his wife and children the great reverse which had befallen them. He had seemed sufficient for them in past years, but after all he had made a mess of both his own life and theirs. He had brought them up for a station which they were not called upon to fill; he had disqualified them from being ordinary working men and women, and he greatly feared that he could do little or nothing to atone for the injury he had inflicted where he had meant to confer the greatest benefit. He had been forgetful in his prosperity that he was growing more than middle-aged, and all these tokens of time in the rooms, which were beating and ticking and striking around him, seemed only there to remind him that the afternoon shadows had fallen across his path, and that though he would gladly employ what was left of it in toiling to make another business, and earn a fresh fortune for his children to spend, soon little more than the evening of life would remain to him. He could not bring back the past and live again the young, strong life, in which hardship and self-denial and work which might have tried a horse were burdens easy to carry, in the light of the confidence which had never been dashed and the hope that had known no disappointment.

All the time Eppie was lying 'waukrife' (wakeful) by his side, not stirring an inch, hardly daring to breathe, in case she should waft away that downy sleep of which she was persuaded her husband stood greatly in need. She only took it upon her to remonstrate—in vain, though she was at the same time slightly reassured by his making the exertion and by the determination with which he persisted in it—when he would rise betimes, even earlier than his usual hour.

It was a fine September morning, and Tam strolled out upon the terrace, before breakfast, and looked about him. Yonder lay his bleach-fields, with the dew glittering upon the whiteness, into which all the rainbow colours were merged at this distance. The inhabitants of the thriving village, the roofs of which were just visible beyond the tree-tops of Barley Riggs, were dependent upon these fields and the adjoining works for their daily bread. How would it fare with them when his rule was at an end? Would the long 'offisher lad' Mackinnon, with the drawling tongue and the indifferent manner, into whose hands Drysdale Haugh must fall, make anything of it— make more of it than his father had made? What chance was there? Not the most distant.

What retribution was this that had come upon him, Tam Drysdale? He had never willingly wronged a Mackinnon of them; for that matter he had never, with his knowledge and by his consent, injured any human being. He had sought all his life to help his neighbours as he had helped himself. He had exerted himself to save the old Miss Mackinnons from starvation, which their precious grand-nephew had been too supercilious a puppy so much as to conceive of, and present a sufficient shield between the women who had reared him and a beggar's death. Auld Tam had interposed a second time to deliver the ladies from the consequences of their trespass against the law of the land, and had striven his hardest to rescue them, else they might have been transported beyond the seas at this day, grey-headed gentlewomen though they were, without their cipher of a gentleman nephew being able to help it.

And what had been Tam Drysdale's reward? That he had planned and laboured and built and improved, for Guy Mackinnon's son to enter upon Tam's labours, and reap the fruits of the harvest his father had wasted and sold for his ease and pleasure—as much as ever Esau had sold his birthright for a mess of pottage. Shall not the Judge of all the earth do right? Yet He had allowed the legality of Esau's deed, while He was going to annul Gavin Mackinnon's. The God of Bethel had upheld Jacob after he had sought to clinch his bargain by a barefaced deception, practised on a blind old man—his own father; but He would forsake Tam Drysdale. Tam was at the bottom of his heart a sincerely religious man; but, as often happens, in the great trial of his life his faith was assailed by such violent gusts of doubt and despair as threatened to tear the plant up by the roots, and leave it to wither and be burnt like any worthless weed of accident and habit.

Near at hand the early morning sun was glinting on the ivy, shrouding the bit of the building which had belonged to the old farmhouse—the dwelling of that earlier Drysdale against whom Tam had hitherto borne no grudge for transferring his property through Beenie Pryde and Maggie Craig to the Mackinnons. Tam had considered that the man had a right to do what he liked with his own, and that Tam's unfortunate father had justly forfeited any claim of kinship. On the whole, Tam had preferred that he should win back what had belonged to his progenitors by his individual industry and ability, so that it might be doubly his. But now, he felt as if his father's cousin had been in a conspiracy to betray him to the Mackinnons, to enable them not only to get their own out of him, but to serve themselves for long years after he had ceased to be their servant with his sinews and brains—to end by robbing him of his best, under no plea except that he had taken what they had not prized, what they had actually tendered for his acceptance, without the right to do so.

On this side of the terrace were the offices and gardens on which their master had bestowed such pains, where his beasts were lodged like Christians, and his flowers were the finest in the west-country—for Eneas Mackinnon to boast of. Great beds of gorgeous autumn dahlias, and tall hollyhocks, untouched as yet by frost, had been so arranged that the gazer from the terrace could catch a glimpse of their wealth of size and colour, and Tam, walking there only yesterday morning, had wondered if the hanging gardens of Damascus had held anything more stately and splendid.

As auld Tam looked, young Eppie came tripping out in her fresh morning-gown, calling upon her father to praise her for her early rising, asking if he would not go with her to the orchid-house, which he had not seen since Neil had done stocking it; and did he know Neil said the dwarf apricot and peach trees, which he had kept back and was now to put under glass, would provide the table with peaches and apricots all the winter, and that the silver sand and peat mould had answered so well with the rhododendrons, next spring the heads would be as big as cabbages. Did he think it could be true that he would beat Lady Semple and everybody at the next year's flower-shows?

Auld Tam was restless to set off to Glasgow to his office, though he had a sense beforehand that there, as here, not only would the glory be departed, he would look at everything with the eyes of a doomed man. He would feel like the dying man on whom the irrevocable sentence has passed, that within a period longer or shorter, measured in this instance by a refinement of torture with his own hand, he must go forth and be no longer seen, while the place which had known him, where he had been happy and honoured, would know him no more.

Tam wondered, as he drove through the streets, who would miss him, and for how long they would speak of his rise and fall,

SUSPICION BECOMES CERTAINTY.

as he had heard other histories spoken of, half as an encouragement, half as a warning. He passed into his office, the brass plate on the door bearing 'Messrs. Thomas Drysdale & Son' still showing the last two words freshly cut in the metal. He received the usual respectful greetings as if he were in some sort a stranger there already, though nobody else knew it—as if the greetings, were not intended for him, but for another person, so that there was a species of mockery in his accepting them.

Still, auld Tam was strong enough to make no sign which anyone save a woman like Eppie the elder, with the intuition of love and the nearness to the object of her scrutiny which she commanded, could have detected. Even young Tam was not aware that there was anything amiss with his father. More than once, as the hours passed by, the younger man admired the acuteness of perception and the grasp both of present details and future results which the head of the firm showed in negotiating sundry extensive transactions that came in the course of the day's work. For, fairly launched in the full swing of his engagements, Tam rid himself of every paralyzing abstraction that had seized hold of him, and was, if anything, more alert and earnest in business than ever, as if the prosperity of Drysdale and Son depended upon how he discharged his customary duties.

According to what was no infrequent occurrence in auld Tam's experience, appeals were made to him on behalf of others engaged in the same business, and where the interests of trade in general and of some of the municipal affairs of the city were concerned. He was asked to pronounce on the dealings of strangers, to give his opinion on clashing theories; he was invited to take an active part in one of the political questions which was reckoned of vital moment to the welfare of his townsmen, and never had the decisions, which were listened to with such flattering attention, struck the hearers as shrewder, sounder, more unbiased, more worthy of the man.

That day's programme was a sample of many such programmes, for still auld Tam put off taking action on the discovery he had made. As he had said to himself that it was not a step to take on the spur of the moment, he went on to say it was not a step to take on a week or a month's notice. A man must have time to set his house in order—such a great house as Tam had reared and was about to pull down—to think and plan if nothing could be done to render the overthrow less complete, to seek the first legal advice in the country, as Tam had been prone to do in matters of much less moment, and ascertain if there were no honourable way out of the labyrinth. Yet all the time Tam sickened at the thought of law and lawyers, and he did not believe that there could be any loophole for escape. His common-sense, stimulated by the hints Mr. Greig had given him, convinced the proprietor of Drysdale Haugh that marriage contracts, about which he had thought so little, must be made for the most part in the interest of the children of the contracting parties, to preserve to them their inheritance, and that no tampering with such legal obligations could be permitted.

Thus, though Tam told himself that he was waiting to consult the foremost lawyers, the consultation too was deferred until all at once he began to ask himself, with a certain fierceness in the question, whether he were called upon to sacrifice himself and all he held dear. His Eppie, young Tam, and the rest; his earnings, his reputation, his trade; 'these sheep' over at the works, who would suffer in a hundred ways from being consigned to incapable hands—all to undo the consequences of a negligence to which Tam could not deny that he had been a party, but with regard to which he had certainly been the least guilty. If he obeyed the dictates of a scrupulous conscience, a gross injustice would be committed. The child of the principal offender, who could never have missed what he had never possessed or dreamt of possessing, and would not know what to do with if it were laid at his feet, would reap a huge profit from the wrong done by his father and mother against him and his neighbour.

After Tam had landed himself in this moral quagmire, a new torment beset him. He was haunted by the presence of Sandy Macnab, the dog-man at Semple Barns. Go where Tam liked, in the streets of Glasgow, on the country roads near Drysdale Hall and Semple Barns, Sandy Macnab was constantly turning up promiscuously very much in the fashion of a fatality. Of course Tam, in his distempered frame of mind, was liable to exaggerate the accident; nevertheless it existed. Naturally the sight of Sandy, with the recollections it conjured up, was not from the first agreeable to Tam. As time progressed, and the workings of his mind had reached a certain stage, they began, in spite of him, to present the strapping, easy-minded, thick-skinned Highlander in the light of an accomplice forced upon Tam's notice. Before long the merest glimpse of the muscular figure, with the erect, almost martial, gait and elastic step, the swarthy complexion, the roving eye, the fluttering tartans, became perfectly detestable to the person who had once been full of a fine serenity, but was fast growing fidgety, testy, and disposed to consider himself impertinently intruded upon.

Rather inexplicably, Sandy, who could not be depended upon for fine feelings, had shown, to begin with, considerable sympathy with auld Tam's aversion to encountering him. Sandy, too, had given signs of trouble at the persistent luck by which he came across the master of Drysdale Hall in these recent days. It boded no good to either—according to the Highlander's superstitious fancies. To be always running up against a gentleman was a token that you and he had something more than either of you guessed, perhaps, to do with each other—something in common to answer for, it might be; and if so, that retribution was already dogging your steps.

So Sandy also had practised looking another way and making a pretence of not seeing his master's friend. But this becoming shyness and reserve had not lasted for any length of time. After a short interval Sandy Macnab rather sought to attract Tam's attention, and made various overtures to speak with him—not without a hateful mysteriousness that defeated its object. Tam resisted indignantly. He was not sunk to this, that he should have Sandy Macnab for his confidant, and live at his mercy. Far better let the man tell the little he knew in whatever quarter he liked, and anticipate the announcement which auld Tam was never sure that he might not make any day. He only questioned its righteousness with a sore questioning, and waited till he could satisfy himself of its propriety; but he would take no blackguard precautions to conceal the contract which had come by no act of his into his hands, which he might have de-destroyed the moment he understood its real bearing, and nobody been any wiser. It would have been time enough then to make terms with a groom and dog-man, a forward, swaggering hanger-on of the gentry; a thick-sculled whelp like Sandy Macnab. But instead, the paper lay, safe and untampered with, in the desk in Tam's business-room, ready for him to produce any day, and to pass on, as he had meant on receiving it, to 'the offisher lad Mackinnon.'

After the casual encounters had come to have the air of Sandy Macnab's being regularly on the outlook for Tam, though the Highlander's general deportment was not so much insolently aggressive as shamefacedly anxious, and as if he had something on his mind to impart; and after the man had advanced more than once with a scrape of a bow and an apologetic 'Gude-day to you, Mr. Drysdale, if you please, sir——-' and Tam had brushed past with a short nod, or an answering 'Gude-day to you, Macnab—another time, I'm engaged,' delivered unwillingly and briefly, the interruption became more serious. Sandy would not be so easily dismissed; he stood his ground and persistently pressed for a hearing. 'I maun have a word wi' you, Mr. Drysdale; I'll not keep you a moment.'

'You can have no word with me,' forbade Tam, sternly and rudely. 'Man, do you not see I'm about my proper business?' (the colloquy was in a street in Glasgow); 'I'm not to be stopped by a carle like you.'

It was the first time that auld Tam had exhibited his ascent in the social scale by employing an opprobrious term and behaving with arrogance to a social inferior. He had been wont to show himself markedly civil, even gentle, towards the class to which he had formerly belonged. He was losing his manners as well as his tranquillity in his tribulation.

'But it's about Rory, sir,' Sandy explained hurriedly, in an impressive undertone.

'What have I to do with your Rories?' protested Tam, in a sudden, unreasoning fury. 'He may gang to the deevil if he likes, and you too; it is no business of mine. You know you did me out of a sum of money because a daft caird [mad tramp] in the country you hail from had a parcel of stolen auld papers—which were nothing to me—that he had travelled sooth with, expecting me, or some other fule with money in his pockets, to buy them. That I was so far left to mysel' is no warrant for you to waylay me in the open street and pester me about a rogue and vagabond. If he had gotten his deserts I should have handed him over to the police, with you in his company. Stand out of my road, sir, or I'll speak to Sir Jeames about this nuisance.'

Sandy Macnab gave way instantly, looking not so much indignant as confounded, which he well might be.

'Is the honest man in a frenzy?' he asked himself. 'Sir Jeames, when he has risen aff his wrong side, is nothing to him. Yet I've aye heard that this bleacher billie [fellow] was a douce chiel and easy to deal with. I did not find him so ill to get on wi' when I gave him a ca' at his place; no, though puir Rory was maist rampageous, and the gentleman was a thocht hard upon me for maistering the craytur. Where would he have been without me? I'm thinking I've stood his friend from first to last, though I may have put my fit into the business this time. Is't siller that makes the gentleman—auld Tam as they ca' him—neither to haud nor to bind when his contered [crossed], or is it because he cam' out of the gutter? I'm thinking it maun be the last, for his son, that is his partner and maun have the pouch [purse] in his turn, is a ceevil enough spoken lad. He will have learned the manners of gentlemen, and not care to rage like a bull of Bashan when there is no occasion for it. If there had been cause the thing would have been different. A man can forgie a round of curses when there is sufficient provocation. It's a faut that the highest in the land may fa' into without prejudice. But just because he was asked with a' respect to stand still and lend an ear, it is preposterous. Weel, I've dune my best to make a clean briest and quiet Bawby Sed's wake mind, but a wilfu' man maun have his way, and if ill come of it the wyte's [blame's] none of mine.'

Sandy Macnab ceased from that day to thrust himself on Tam's notice or to crave speech with him; but the incident had made a painful impression, which rankled in Tam's memory. Among all the misery of this time he could not shake off the apprehension that the annoyance would repeat itself—that it had a motive which he had yet to fathom.

CHAPTER XXXII.

IN THE BALANCE.

THE world went on much the same this autumn, though everything under the sun was altered to Tam Drysdale, as he knew. The slight sprinkling of grey, which had been all that had appeared formerly in his brown hair, was on the road to become a heavy powdering of white.

A wistful light had crept into the happy eyes of the elder Eppie, which were now so often resting, as she would have said, stowlins [by stealth] on her husband. Her rampant prosperity was subdued by a hidden sorrow. Something was wrong with her Tam which she could not divine; she only knew that he did not come to her for consolation; so she supposed the evil, whatever it might be, was beyond her power of alleviation, and she was silently sorry, with a meek devoted woman's unscorning, ungrudging pity.

Mrs. Drysdale was not half so fine or nearly so ridiculous as she had been. What did she care for finery when there was something amiss with Tam? And as she ceased to pay heed to the good things of her position, and the suitable deportment they called for from her, her vulgarity was toned down, and she lost much of her self-consciousness and superficial affectation. A new charm was added to her other attractions. Something like the dawning of dignity—the dignity of indifference to the accidents of circumstance, and of a soul occupied by higher things—began to show itself in Eppie. But these were subtle signs, and they were the sole indication that anything had happened; though they might be indirectly felt, they were not distinctly recognised.

Drysdale Hall was, to all outward appearance, the same as it had ever been since it was created by its present owner; and since young Tam and Clary had grown up, bringing with them fresh life and movement—animated, full of the thrills and throbs of passion in natures endowed with the strength and ardour of their early prime, even while it was most divergent and discordant where the general current was concerned. And now a new figure in the second generation—young Eppie, in her simplicity and sweetness, was hovering on the threshold of that flight into the world which boys and girls must take sooner or later.

As the tides obey the moon, so do the lower strata of society answer to the higher, though the distance between them is more or less great, and there are no conspicuous points of union. Because Parliament is up, and London deserted by the upper ten thousand in September, so those who are not in Parliament, and have nobody connected with them affected by its sitting and rising, choose that season when the daylight is beginning to shorten and the moderate heat to cool, when wild flowers are mostly gone and birds have ceased to sing, for their annual holiday and their sojourn in the country. Rural resorts which have no call to answer to the necessities of legislators become inundated with temporary residents who have not even the excuse of being bandsters [binders of corn], or theekers [thatchers] of stacks, or peripatetic owners of thrashing-machines, and are callous to all the delights of June with her long days and broomy braes, and July with her meridian heat, her bluebells by the wayside, and her dog-roses in the hedgerows. But there is one glory gilding the fall of the year, that exists alike for gentle and simple of the more combative sex. It is not compelled by the breaking-up of Parliament, the partial closing of Government offices, the vacations of the law courts, though it does much in its turn to compel these pauses in the business of the country. The name of this potent charmer is 'Sport,' which reigns from the 12th of August to the last hunt of the advancing spring. The enchantress is rampant in her sway when the moors, the turnip-fields, the coverts, are possessed by an army of men in shooting-jackets, with staghounds and pointers for their allies, and the air is full of the bang of small artillery.

St. Mungo's City is not an exception to the rest of the world, in the desire to kill the beautiful wild creatures of the hills and the fields. After Glasgow has poured her swarms 'down the water,' in early summer, she sends fresh swarms of the wealthier grades to render the heather and the stubble alive with more than deer and grouse, hares and pheasants. Autumn always brought a pleasant excitement of company and gaiety to Drysdale Hall, with crowded breakfast-tables, meetings at the scene of action, open-air luncheons, frequent guests to dinner, little dances when there were enough young people in the house. Doubtless the fashion was borrowed from Semple Barns, where members of Parliament on the wing did alight on occasion, and refresh their nervous systems, exhausted by services to the nation, with tramping through briars and brambles, leaping over ditches, and bringing down partridges.

Auld Tam commanded a little good shooting on his property, and he rented a moor within two hours' journey by railway, on which active men, accustomed both to business and hunting hours, starting with the lark and reaching their destination before the dew was dry on the red ling, could traverse the ground, fill creditable bags, and be back to dinner several times a week, from the 12th to the 1st, when prey nearer home afforded the coveted pursuit without the sacrifice of a railway journey.

Tam Drysdale hardly took his gun in his hand this season, but in the other direction young Tam allowed himself greater indulgence in the natural propensity of the biped that can pull a trigger. The only eccentricity he displayed was that he was quick to share moor and shooting with any of his managers who had taken out licenses, and that the son kept up the father's practice in the disposal of the spoil of his gun. Instead of sending the game to fetch a fair price in the Glasgow poultry-shops, he despatched what did not find its way to the Drysdale Hall larder, to Dr. Peter Murray for distribution among his patients, or to the appreciative wives and families of bleachers and dyers who would otherwise have had little chance of tasting hare or pheasant that was honestly come by.

Young Tam was not left to cope with the fowls of the air and the hares and the rabbits of the pasture single-handed, save for his subordinates or his Glasgow acquaintance who could exchange a shooting with him. Eneas Mackinnon, who was understood to be indebted to his friends for such sport as he got, came over with Dick Semple whenever they were not better employed elsewhere.

A far more brilliant ally arrived in good time. Sir Hugo Willoughby had kept his word. He had reappeared just when he had said he would, and was making himself more popular than ever by declining to herd with his kind and by casting in his lot with the young Glasgow men. In fact, he kept hovering in the immediate vicinity of St. Mungo's City, with its roar of traffic, its smoky abominations, its boisterous superfluity and ostentation. He defied Guy Horsburgh, who began to look uneasy in the office of bear-leader, which he had taken upon himself, to wile him, Sir Hugo, to any distance—to induce him to take a yachting voyage to Iceland or a walking tour in Ross or Sutherland—to try a bout of deer-stalking in any of the deer forests, the tenants of which were friends of his. He would not even go down with Guy to that Court in Lincolnshire which he had often proposed to show to his friend, where Lady Willoughby sat lonely in her castle hall, awaiting her truant son in vain, and where preserves choke-full of all the lowland game which could satisfy the heart of a man or the muzzle of a gun were wasting their sweetness on the desert air, and calling loudly for an absent, inconsiderate squire to diminish the *embarras des richesses*, else he would have a host of farmers, his natural allies, rising up in open rebellion against him. Not above a certain radius of miles would Sir Hugo budge from Glasgow—Glasgow in August and September, not Glasgow down-the-water, fresh with sea and mountain breezes, but Glasgow inland, with her thick carpet of grimy dust and her black pall of filthy smoke—Glasgow squalid, careworn, miserable, when the depression of trade caused the fitful rattle of the machinery to sound eerie and hollow as when slaves shake their chains, and the sweat of men's brows began to gather in the big drops of despair.

There was nothing more terrible to fear save the silence of death, when a great strike testifies to the revolt of one class and the rending asunder of two.

It might have been that young Sir Hugo was so true a philosopher and so promising a patriot that he was bent on becoming acquainted with all shades of life in one of the great trade centres which he had elected to study. But so far as this went, Sir Hugo turned his back on the city and was engrossed with the wonders of his own young existence. At this time he neither knew nor cared much for its sins and sorrows, cherishing a sanguine hope that they would all cure themselves somehow, and be mended by an alchemy with which he had nothing to do. It was the neighbourhood of Glasgow, and not Glasgow itself, to which he was nailed. The Horsburghs had their country-house not far from Drysdale Hall, and though it was the most commonplace of modern dwellings, he was content with it.

Be it said also that Sir Hugo had returned to his first love—to the pursuit of the Cinderella who had fled from him in the Drysdale Hall picture-gallery, the 'young thing, just come frae her mammy,' who had sung to him in the Drysdale Hall drawing-room. He had called Athole Murray charming, but he had forgotten her wit long before he saw her face again. It was the recollection of young Eppie's guileless sweetness, combined with her spring-time loveliness, which he called divine, that had taken fast hold of his mind.

Sir Hugo could not display these inclinations without causing a flutter of marvel and speculation; but first when he came back auld Tam took no further notice of the young man, about whom he had made such a fuss at Easter, than if he had been an ordinary mortal. It seemed as if a benumbing power was at work on the master of Drysdale Hall. He became cold and passive to what would formerly have roused him to hot and strong approbation or opposition. He made no more sign of displeasure at the continued presence of Eneas Mackinnon at Drysdale Hall, than of pleasure at the pertinacity with which Sir Hugo Willoughby seized every opportunity of renewing his visits. Not the lifting of a finger, the flicker of an eyelid, the raising of the voice, uttered an imperative protest when young Tam showed again his exclusive preference for Barley Riggs among the houses of his acquaintance, and, under pretext of watching some chemical experiments conducted by Dr. Peter in his laboratory, spent three evenings of the week there.

It was as if a dull indifference was settling down on auld Tam—a strange insensibility to what had been wont to affect him in the liveliest manner. His wife, who but for him would have been at the height of a mother's mingled pride and pain, quivering with excitement like the youngest hero or heroine among them, whose fortune was hanging in the balance, grew more and more puzzled, chilled, frightened, by Tam's want of sympathy, even of angry interest, in the affairs of his children at what looked like a turning-point in their destiny.

Clary, who had braced herself for a contest—violent while it lasted—had her whole ideas upset by finding that there was apparently to be no altercation—she was to be let alone to go her own ways. It was not an inspiriting change to a woman of her temperament, and she was the next thing to piqued by it. If she had cared only for asserting her will, and had not been thoroughly honest, with a capacity for steadfastness where her affections were placed, she might have been driven to give up Eneas Mackinnon.

As for Eneas, in spite of all the encouragement that a young proud woman could give him, he had been tempted to hang back, in an agony of mortified self-respect, sensitiveness and shame, from the inevitable explanation and the almost equally inevitable accusation of presumption and unworthy motives on his part, which the announcement to auld Tam would call forth. Eneas, too, was dumbfounded, and in some degree overwhelmed by the amnesty that was granted to him. Was he to go on shooting Tam Drysdale's partridges on the land which had belonged to Eneas's mother, eating auld Tam's dinners—the usual end to the day's shootings—making love to his beautiful capable daughter, with her free consent, under her father's very nose, or was Eneas to fail Claribel and withdraw at the last moment, vanquished by the strange trust put in him?

Young Tam was lordlier in his behaviour. He acted as if he did not see that his father had any right to dispose of his son's spare time or modify his taste for this or that company. He made no bones of going over to Barley Riggs. He did not condescend to the smallest concealment. He had even the coolness to borrow his father's lantern on a dark rainy night, looking auld Tam in the face as the son proffered the request, telling the owner where the light was to guide the willing feet that scouted a carriage, and were ready to trudge through wind and rain to reach their goal.

'Tak' the lantern, laddie. You'll find it in the harness-room,' said Tam gruffly, but without boiling over, without even wincing, though he let his head drop a little on his breast.

Was nothing else worth caring for so long as that thing hung over his head? Might his children all come and go—they for whom he had striven, who were as the apple of his eye, whom not so long ago he would fain have curbed and bent to force them into other channels than those they had formed for themselves, for the lad and lass's good? Could they do as they liked for anything their father cared, he was so hopeless and heartless for them, for himself, for the whole world?

Dr. Peter, in wholesome unconscious ness, was as blind as ever; and all that Athole Murray did was to laugh at young Tam till the tears came into her own eyes, to twit him with his opinions and performances, to shut herself up with her patterns, pets, and books, and excuse herself from coming to see the retorts, disappointing both of the operators—to keep away from Drysdale Hall and every other place where she was likely to encounter the young man.

But Athole was beginning to meet her match. Tam the younger was fast outgrowing that sour effervescence of greenness and youth to which Dr. Peter had once alluded. The junior partner in Drysdale and Son's was losing his self-consciousness and susceptibility. He was settling down into calm, strong manhood, knowing what it wanted, and not to be easily turned from seeking to supply its wants. Young Tam was ceasing to mind Athole's flouts. He had advanced so far as to smile at them—

a little grimly, perhaps, but still to smile and go on his way without being in the slightest degree deterred by her bearing. He did not mean to show it, but a certain quiet, far from unhappy masterfulness was stealing into his looks and tones. She did not know that she betrayed it, but a certain humility and nervousness, which were not altogether unhappy either, though the unacknowledged restraint provoked and affronted her, lurked under her most audacious sally and sharpest repartee.

CHAPTER XXXIII.

A DROWNING MAN'S STRAWS.

It was none of the persons chiefly concerned, but a mere looker-on, who, without in the least understanding the case, awoke auld Tam from his lethargy, and gave his troubled mind a new bias.

Lady Semple, with her natural versatility, had long ago renounced her projects for Claribel as the destined Lady Willoughby. Lady Semple had, not without reason, made up her mind instead that Claribel Drysdale ought to marry Mr. Mackinnon. Her father could not really disapprove of the poor match for his elder daughter, else he would not have allowed her to come prominently forward, as she

A DROWNING MAN'S STRAWS.

had come, to the help of the unfortunate old ladies. Nothing would warrant such compromising conduct in a young lady except an attachment, of which, indeed, her ladyship had not been without her suspicions at an earlier date, to be speedily followed by the announcement of an engagement to the grand-nephew.

Lady Semple went on to argue the matter in all its bearings. It was a magnificent instance of mercantile liberality and generosity in a man whom she had always admired and esteemed, whom she was proud to call her friend as well as her neighbour. It would be a splendid thing for Dick's friend — an interposition of Providence on his behalf and the making of him. And it was quite a romance on Claribel's part. Lady Semple herself was not romantic, but when wealthy parents countenanced romance the principal objection to it was removed, and the most prudent third person might follow suit without compunction.

Lady Semple would certainly stand by Claribel when she was Mrs. Mackinnon, both for the sake of Dick and his friend, and because of her ladyship's regard for the young lady. There would be no loss of prestige for her, since the poorest officer's wife would rank with the daughter of the richest dyer and cotton-printer any day; and Mr. Drysdale's money would not come amiss, though unluckily promotion was no longer to be bought. The thinker meant unluckily only in this instance; she was an advanced Liberal in politics, and had been almost as anxious for the abolition of the purchase system as for vote by ballot, though she knew it would be a blow to a number of her nephews. Dick was an only son, and he would soon leave the army; he had only adopted it *pour passer le temps,* and because all men were the better of being trained to a profession— she would say a trade, if she had her way.

The Mackinnons—Mr. Mackinnon and

his wife—would probably continue in the army; but if her father settled a regular income upon her, as a man of his sense and kindness was sure to do, it would not signify much although he never got beyond the rank of a captain or major. She did not suppose he would pass higher by merit, though he was a thoroughly good fellow, fit to be a general where a man's tone rather than his talent was concerned. He would make a good steady husband. She had always been glad that Dick had chosen such a safe friend. Claribel would see the world with her husband's regiment, in which she would be a great force; though it was bad form now to talk of the belle of a regiment—all that had gone out with promotion by purchase and idle young men with their practical jokes, pigeon-shooting, and regimental balls. It was out of date even in fast novels. Officers had now their work to do if they wished to get on like other men, which was much better for them. But Claribel would not be tied down. She would have the opportunity of learning at first hand a variety of things which she, Lady Semple, had missed mastering. She was tempted to envy her young friend.

What would Sir Hugo do? Oh, Sir Hugo had found out that for himself, and it was the most delightful solution possible of the difficulty. He would woo and win young Eppie—the simplest, most artless of little girls. She was so young, that she could be easily trained, while her transference to polite circles would have a thousand times more novelty and charm than Claribel's transplantation could have had. It would be a genuine romance— though Lady Semple was not in the least romantic, any more than Eppie was a beggar-maid. Still, Sir Hugo was a King Cophetua in his way, and only the knowledge of what a dear daughter the young girl, who was devoted to her own good rustic mother, would make to darling unworldly Lady Willoughby, with her widowed life and her devotion to her son, could fully reconcile Lady Semple to the *mésalliance*.

Then Mr. and Mrs. Drysdale need not be left alone. That Trojan of a son of theirs—who had resisted her ladyship's blandishments and those of the Vaughan girls, who had given in to his father by going into business—had become, as she had heard, auld Tam's right hand. He ought to bring over that independent, original Miss Murray, the daughter of clever, innocent Dr. Peter. She was a girl whom Lady Semple was dying to know better. She might be of the greatest assistance to her ladyship in getting up her Rational Dress Association. Athole would prove a fair substitute for the loss of Claribel to her friend, as well as for the double loss of Claribel and Eppie to their parents.

Having arrived at this triumphant conclusion, Lady Semple felt so sure of her ground that she could not imagine herself making mischief by putting in her oar. She first tried a series of broad hints to

Mrs. Drysdale. But Mrs. Eppie was so engrossed with the prospect of the fulfilment of her dreams, so distracted between freshly awakened tenderness for Clary, trembling exultation over young Eppie, vexation with young Tam, and trouble about auld Tam, that, candid woman though she was, it seemed impossible to draw an admission from her, as a step towards offering her friendly congratulations.

Thus foiled, Lady Semple, in her high satisfaction, ventured to have recourse to auld Tam.

It was one evening when the whole *dramatis personæ* of Lady Semple's genteel comedy were together in the old-fashioned drawing-room at Semple Barns. So most of them had been on a previous evening, when Tam Drysdale's eyes had been opened to the enormity of a penniless officer of the Mackinnon stock having rendered himself so agreeable to Clary that he had melted her pride and disordered her understanding, and when her father had scowled on the couple, and angrily told his wife that he would not have such doings.

The summer had done Sir James good, and he was able to meet company. He had quite a knot of old friends—from London, from Edinburgh (where the Court of Session was up, like the Parliament in London), from India, helping Dick to dispose of the birds. Lady Semple had her neighbours and friends to meet the greater strangers: the Drysdales—the whole of them on this occasion; Dr. Peter and Athole Murray, whom her hostess was so desirous of cultivating; Sir Hugo Willoughby, with Guy Horsburgh; Eneas Mackinnon, with the son of the house.

Lady Semple was an accomplished hostess, but her skill was wasted this evening, for her guests gave her little trouble; they arranged themselves according to their own wishes, and hers, without an effort. The old friends mustered round Sir James's card-table, which he could again enjoy, enlivening the pauses during the deals by reminiscences of the past, extracts from their intermediate experience, anticipations of the next day's sport.

Round games for young people were exploded, but there had been an attempt to try the last play of thought-reading, which had only broken down because nobody seemed to care to have his or her thought read; everybody seemed to be more anxious to ascertain his or her neighbour's.

Eneas Mackinnon wanted to learn what Claribel Drysdale was thinking as she inspected the condition of that oddest of sentimental souvenirs—a hair album, which Lady Semple had once set up.

Sir Hugo Willoughby desired to penetrate what had been young Eppie's fancies as the liquid notes of her voice, which she had been pouring forth at the piano, near which he was hovering, died away. A few moments ago she had silenced the whole murmur of sound. The great roomful of old and young, grave and gay, married and single, men and women of the world, and men and women whom nothing would make worldly, had listened breathlessly to the expression of the simple faith of a homely, hardworking breadwinner for some poor family:

> 'When Jock and Jean and Janetie,
>   Are up and gotten lear,
> They'll help to mak' the boatie row,
>   And lighten a' our care.
> Then weel may the boatie row,
>   And better may it speed,
> And weel may the boatie row
>   That wins the bairnies' breed.'

But surely even Eppie, with the clear mirror of her innocent mind unruffled by a cloud of passion, must have a conception of the time when Jock and Jean and Janetie were not only up and had 'gotten lear,' but entertained dreams and a life of their own apart from the visions and the life of the most loving of parents—when the children were in train to fulfil the Bible prophecy, that a man will leave father and mother and cleave to his wife.

Young Tam sought to realize what Athole Murray meant when she told with such merry eloquence to Dr. Peter, in the younger man's hearing, her determination to set agoing a *Haus Chronik*, such as she had read of in a German book. It was to be a Home Chronicle of which the pages stood for the years of her life. She would put the leading scene of the year by means of pencil and brush on the appointed page. For instance, her father's being thrown by Lady Fair when the train went across Aytoun Brig; or herself finding the old iron pot in the garden, which had formed such a delicious study of rusty-brown ever since. Another incident might be Jeannie's refusing the baker's man at the kitchen-door; because if Jeannie had said 'Yes, if you please,' the domestic economy of Barley Riggs would have sustained a severe shock. Oh! he need not think that nobody would understand her compositions, or be the wiser for them, because she was to write in old characters—now her handwriting was fairly readable in modern, so it need not be wholly illegible in old characters—

the details of that annual great event, so that he who ran could read and be instructed.

Would Jeannie and the baker's man be the only couple who were to figure in the Barley Riggs Home Chronicle, if it ever had a being save in Athole's busy brain? and must the scene always be a dismissal?

Mrs. Drysdale also was looking across at her husband, as if to ask him the reason why he drew apart from the other elderly man present, and stood with his hands behind his back gazing, not on the card-table, but on vacancy.

The husband and wife did not look so much *au fait* to each other's minds as they had once looked to a comical extent, or so inclined to refer to each other. The change might easily be when there was such an inroad of exciting elements into their family life, on which it was just possible the couple might hold different views.

Anyhow, matrimonial confidences were not desirable in general company; so Lady Semple adroitly got rid of the matron by sending Dick to pay her a little attention, and herself tried to 'tackle' auld Tam. She went up to him as he moved on, until he stood before a picture of Dick Semple when a boy on his pony, which the critic had contemplated a hundred times.

Lady Semple made the portrait the text of her remarks. 'Do you see any resemblance still, Mr. Drysdale? Oh, these boys and girls, how they run away from us, and how hard it is for us fathers and mothers to be left behind!'

'Mr. Dick is not going to run away from you, mem.'

Tam gave the general observation an individual application with stupid literalness.

'Oh no! not Dick—not yet awhile, I hope,' said his mother hastily; 'though he no longer thinks his father's word law, and his mother's praise does not send him to bed as happy as a king—and it will come to that soon—that other going away from us, and settling in life on his own account, which seems to sunder so many ties. Yet what would you have, Mr. Drysdale?' continued her ladyship, unconsciously adopting the same line of argument which Mrs. Drysdale had formerly used; 'we cannot stand in our children's way. We cannot stay with them always, so why should we seek to keep them with us? It is better—though it is not altogether pleasant, is it?—that they should leave us. But where everybody is agreed, where everything is more than suitable,' murmured Lady Semple, 'where the whole arrangements are simply charming, and there is so much to rejoice at, to be truly thankful for, I can only wish you joy, my dear sir.'

Tam looked up amazed, uncertain, when, as if they were passing before him in a panorama, the groups around him caught his eye in quick succession. His glance roamed from one to another, comprehensively, conclusively. There was a twitch of his eyebrows, he compressed his lips and thrust his chin a little forward in his eagerness to see what was happening. His eyes were still a little dazzled, but they were no longer incapable of receiving a vivid impression. He had shaken off the brown study which had engrossed him; a new idea had come to him; he was full of it and of how it might help him in his strait. But he only said to Lady Semple:

'Not so fast, my leddy, mem—joy is not to be wished every day; we keep it for great occasions.'

'But you own it is only a question of time. Oh, I must wish you much joy, Mr. Drysdale!' cried Lady Semple, enchanted to find herself, as she supposed, correct in what she had conjectured, inclined to look upon the contemplated result as accomplished, feeling as if she had made all these marriages, and that each marriage was in its own way a feat to be proud of. But she had the discretion not to urge Tam further, and to leave him to digest in peace the meal she had provided for him.

It was a meal, under the circumstances. Lieutenant Mackinnon and Clary! Auld

Tam remembered what he had thought of that connection before, but now all the reasons against it were more than annulled. If he gave Clary to young Mackinnon, with the fortune that he might yet hope to bestow, supposing that he were left to grapple with, overcome, and outlive the bad times, without the horrible necessity of having to give back Drysdale Haugh to Mackinnon, with such fines and forfeits in addition as would have shaken the prosperity of the best-established firm in Glasgow—would it not compensate, not for inadvertently depriving him of his mother's property, which might well be forgiven, but for the iniquity of retaining it, after he —auld Tam—knew full well it was none of his? What would 'the offisher lad' have more than the girl he loved, or ought to love, from his pretensions—and Clary was a fine lass, 'handsome and edicate,' a lass to act for herself and him too, a boon to any man, far more than a match for the stick of a lad she had set her fancy on?

And what would the like of young Mackinnon do with Drysdale Haugh if he got it? Make a mess of it, as his father had done before him; waste all that auld Tam had brought the place to; pull down everything that he had built up, and be glad in the end to rid himself of the inheritance, and sell it to some poor, ambitious chiel who could put his hand to the plough like one whom auld Tam had known, as Gavin Mackinnon had sold it.

But Mackinnon and Clary were not the only couple. There was young Tam hanging like a bee about a flower on that 'braw, clever, ill-faured lass,' Athole Murray. Well, the Murrays were mixed up with the old transaction, which loomed so largely in Tam's mind that it blotted out every other. The Murrays had to do with the selling of the works to Tam Drysdale, in spite of the marriage contract which held them for the issue of Margaret Craig. Tam had been hammering his brains all these weeks, in vain, to determine how much or how little the Murrays were involved, and what he had to answer for to them. Dr. Peter's father, Gavin Mackinnon's partner, had been concerned with him in the sale, not of the farm, which had belonged to Mrs. Mackinnon, but of the buildings and plant used in the business, and the business itself, in which he was a partner. Could Murray's descendants also come on Tam for their share in the profits of the dyeing and calico-printing since the sale? On the other hand, could not Tam require from the Murrays their proportion of the purchase-money, which they in their turn might claim from the Mackinnons, since the Murrays also had been misled in the disposal of the business?

It was a complication of interests and injuries which Tam could not unravel. The strong head, which had worked out so many calculations without a throb, ached with the strain. But this he seemed to foresee clearly, that if the matter were laid before Dr. Peter, that upright and uncompromising soul would never rest till he had sifted it to the bottom, and apportioned to every man his due, though in the process a great business might be frittered away, and the capital which the present crisis in trade ought to have appropriated to itself would only be rescued from the wreck, to be parted into fractions of which nobody would be the better except a set of lawyers. Dr. Peter would count any loss in the name of strict integrity well lost.

But if young Tam were 'yoked' with Athole Murray, might not that flea be left to stick in the wall, without any further qualms of conscience? Athole's promotion to be the wife of as fine a fellow as ever lived, the future head of a great business, would far outweigh any debatable advantage the Murrays might gain—not that Tam imagined Dr. Peter greedy of an advantage—by joining with young Mackinnon in compelling Tam to make restitution. And Dr. Peter was a man and a father—his lassie's welfare must be something, must be a great deal to him; if it would not altogether shut his truth-speaking mouth, it must render him more lenient, more manageable, should the real state of the case ever come to light.

Then the marriage would make Tam's lad happy, would atone to him for the loss of his father; for it was one of the most bitter drops infused into auld Tam's full cup, in the tremendous change which had suddenly darkened the broad sunshine of his prosperity, and rendered all his good things worthless to him, to be forced to comprehend that, having found his son, it was only to lose him again. There had been till recently many business confidences between them, in which auld Tam had been proud to think that his hands were clean, and that he had not to soil young Tam's by the contact. He had never dabbled in business ruses which could not bear repetition to uncorrupted ears. But here was an affair which could not stand being looked into, which must remain a secret, and rise up as a barrier between the father and his son for the term of their lives. Very likely, if the story chanced to be approached—and what secret was not approached sooner or later?—it would demand more sacrifices from him of deliberate, habitual deception and brazen falsehood to maintain the central lie. How could he look young Tam in the face if it were so, when the father had begun already in his misery to skulk away from one of the creatures he loved best in the world? And he had a full-hearted, despairing conviction that young Tam, hot-headed as he had been, independent as he was, would miss his father's friendship, little worth as it was—would want a perfect mate in a wife, the desire of his heart, to make up to him for the snapping of the primitive tie which, when it is of true metal, is of the consistency of iron.

Last of all, there was Tam Drysdale's youngest child, his bonnie bairn Eppie, with the splendid prospect of marrying

Sir Hugo Willoughby, and being removed far beyond the range of commercial storms, safely landed among the aristocracy, in the august shadow of the Throne itself, as Tam dreamed. If he could only hold out till that achievement was accomplished, till little Eppie's grand fortune was secured, and her mother left to her care, for young Eppie would never see her mother suffer, then he could be content to die—not in peace—this was not a question of peace, but stubborn and silent. For what had auld Tam done that he should demolish his name and fame and ruin his children to enrich Gavin Mackinnon's son? But he would enrich Gavin Mackinnon's son, and what more could be required of him?

CHAPTER XXXIV.

AULD TAM 'FEY.'

AULD TAM came out of his shell in a fever of forced spirits, with a restless desire to be doing something. It looked like a boisterous, nearly wild gaiety, which caused his friends to stare and almost to stand aghast. Tam would again get up extravagant entertainments for Sir Hugo, who had by this time made himself so much at home at Drysdale Hall, that it was a bore to him to be treated like a comparative stranger, and ranked still as a guest.

But Tam would have entertained the whole world in his present frame of mind; anything was sufficient for an excuse to bring people together, to establish general good-fellowship, to give ample opportunities of meeting and settling matters, to individuals who hankered after such encounters. The *raison d'être* was to force on the business in hand, till what might have tarried and languished, been blighted by unexpected contrary winds and perished in spite of its early promise, was brought to a swift, irresistible conclusion.

The master of Drysdale Hall was not satisfied with ordinary entertainments. He cudgelled his brains and scoured the city and country for something to show, something to visit, something to make merry over. Auld Tam blossomed all at once into being the patron of half-a-dozen societies, demanding dinners and suppers and balls from their munificent patron, with Drysdale Hall for the headquarters of such members as were pressed into the service of these feasts.

Notwithstanding plenty of evidence that Guy Horsburgh had long ago enabled Sir Hugo Willoughby to 'do' Glasgow thoroughly, Tam was struck with a sudden patriotic zeal lest any place should have been passed by. He insisted on making up parties of a heterogeneous description, including all and sundry, among them the oppressed Sir Hugo, to 'do' Glasgow over again — engineers' shops, sugar-refiners' premises, cotton-mills, without mercy—the whole at an unpropitious epoch. And the sightseers were sure to return in a body to profit by the lavish hospitality of Drysdale Hall, grown excessive to the exercising the soul of the housekeeper and the wearying of the spirit of Mrs. Drysdale. There might have been no such thing as bad trade, to judge from the joviality and regardlessness of domestic expenses which auld Tam was exhibiting.

A launch was announced in one of the shipyards, to which Tam not only had access, but was complimented by being asked to let one of his family name the vessel. He consented readily, giving the honour to Clary, and at the last moment bidding Mr. Mackinnon guide her arm, which was steady enough in itself. But Eneas's hand shook in the duty confided to him, till Claribel told him reproachfully if she had not been firmer than he was, he would have caused her to swerve in her aim, and dash the bottle of wine against the stays instead of the side of the vessel, so that the good ship *Claribel* must have gone forth unchristened and luckless to meet her fate on the high seas.

Auld Tam took to coveting more pictures for his gallery, and, losing faith in his native discernment and considerable experience, sallied forth, accompanied by a train of people, to consult on the merits of the pictures for sale in a west-country gallery which had come to the hammer. Very probably Tam was right that, after himself, Athole Murray was the best judge among his motley followers. But he deferred to her till her ears, which she could not believe, began to tingle, her teeth were set on edge, and she was reduced to talking nonsense, when he bought the worst picture in the lot on her jesting recommendation. Immediately afterwards, in the hearing of everybody, he presented the picture to young Tam as the 'handsel' to a new room which had been fitted up for him. Why, young Tam gaped, even as Athole's face fell, grew white, and took an absolutely scared look.

Auld Tam became as incapable of buying flowers as of purchasing pictures unsupported by a circle of friends, while he refused to delegate the commission to his head-gardener. Tam summoned the two Eppies, Athole Murray, and Clary if she chose, to attend him to the West of Scotland Autumn Flower Show, and signified graciously to the young men within earshot of the arrangement that if they had an eye for 'geranums' and 'gladioly' they might look in at the show and repair to Ferguson's for luncheon afterwards. Sir Hugo at least looked in and praised the display up to the skies, all because of a certain Scotch rose which was infinitely captivating to him. Young Eppie was struck by a new pelargonium, of which not only did her father buy many specimens from the nurseryman who was its fortunate introducer, but Sir Hugo was convinced that it would be a great addition to the geraniums at Willoughby Court, and that his mother would like the variety immensely. He, too, bought largely, when the seller, apprised of the rank of his customer and full of visions of his geraniums becoming the fashion in the great world, paid the same compliment to Sir Hugo that the shipbuilder had paid to auld Tam. The nurseryman offered the young English baronet the name of the yet nameless flower. Sir Hugo hesitated, and glanced from the one to the other with sparkling eyes and a word trembling on the tip of his tongue. He was as modest as he was ingenuous, and he was too deep in the toils to be quite free to pay compliments. Still a flower, like a star, was a beautiful namesake, fit for his Scotch rose, destined, perhaps, to hand down her name to a floral immortality.

Auld Tam saved the young fellow whatever delicate scruple he felt.

'What would you think, Sir Hugie,' said the father insinuatingly, 'to give the name to young Eppie here? She was the first to call our attention to the flower, so that the name is hers, in a sense.'

'A thousand thanks for the permission, Mr. Drysdale,' cried Sir Hugo eagerly. 'Will you do me the honour to grant your consent, Miss Eppie?' speaking with soft emphasis, as if hers were the casting vote; ' shall this happy geranium be linked with you always?'

' Oh, no, no, Sir Hugo!' protested Eppie, in a bashful tumult of mingled pride and humility and instinctive shyness. 'It is not an honour—I mean my name is not an honour. Call the flower after your mother, Lady Willoughby, and then it will be like "Lady Pollock," which has such bonnie leaves. That will be much better. "Eppie" is not a nice name for a flower; it is not half fine enough. I dare say Lady Willoughby would not like it.'

'Excuse me,' said Sir Hugo, beaming, 'you must let me be the judge. My mother likes all that I like. I should be so pleased and proud to have your name associated with anything at Willoughby Court. It is your mother's name also; speak for me, Mrs. Drysdale—you who are good to everybody—that I may send a token of you to my home, and find it flourishing there when I go back.'

'You're ower kind,' Sir Hughie,' said gentle mother Eppie.

At that plea of her mother's name, young Eppie gave in, not without a sense of innocent importance and elation at knowing that there was thenceforth a beautiful flower identified with her, that the 'Eppie' variety of pelargonium, which would no doubt come into general favour, would remain as a remembrance of those happy days. For very happy were those days to Eppie. She was young enough to enjoy with inexhaustible zest, and without any anxiety, the constant excitement. She did not even pause to ask what other delightful glamour of tender flattery, and pleased approval from all around her, was thrown over the time—what it all tended to, and what it all meant.

Tam Drysdale in his rawest youth had never been so idly disposed, so inclined to linger before setting out for Glasgow in the morning, to return to Drysdale Hall in the middle of the day, to seek to infect young Tam with his truancy by proposing to bring his son away from the office or the works hours before the appointed time. It looked as if auld Tam were fain to break through the daily routine of business, in order to pursue pleasure at his age, and that he desired young Tam's countenance in the unbecoming proceeding. The head of the firm replaced the spirit of energy which he had displayed on the back of his unsuspected misfortune by a kind of disgust at the work which had formerly been as marrow to his bones. He accepted every poor excuse for dalliance and distraction. He would even have revived croquet-practice, since he was too heavy and stiff for tennis, if the young people had not laughed and hung back from the slow, old-fashioned diversion, so that he had reason to fear a deficiency of players.

For no manœuvring mother was ever more crafty and persistent in carrying out her drift. In two conspicuous instances it was so incomprehensible to the onlooker, and so opposed to auld Tam's former tactics, that it baffled the shrewdest wit to penetrate it, and remained unsolved. If any mortal had possessed the clue it would have been pitiable to see the strait to which Tam Drysdale was reduced to effect a compromise between honour and dishonour.

Auld Tam's spasmodic attempts at gaiety, his uncouth gambols, culminated in a great 'treat' or feast to his work-people at Drysdale Haugh — to which everybody he knew was invited, and for which he spared no preparations. At his instigation the two Eppies were engaged for a whole day superintending the floral decorations of the room in which Dr. Peter had given his lecture. And the giver of the entertainment went himself and fetched Athole Murray (one of his pattern-designers!)—reluctant, annoyed, with a half-comical, half-hurt and angry sense that though the younger Eppie was glad to see her, the elder was affronted by her presence, and went as near to snubbing her as it was possible for either of the Eppies to snub any human being. The result was that Athole was prompted to be more merciless in her intolerance of young Tam, more savage—as even a kind woman can be savage—in her raillery where he was concerned, than she had shown herself for many a day, and that the revenge was likely to be taken under his mother's indignant, horrified eyes.

There were games, dancing, and a sumptuous supper for Tam's satellites. He had commanded his wife and daughters to appear in full dress, Eppie in her velvet and diamonds, Claribel in her ivory tinted silk and coral, and sweet young Eppie in the very soft pink and silver plumage which Clary had imagined for her. She wore, with great glee, the prettiest little watch in Muirhead's, which her father had given her on her birthday. She was the real queen of the evening, and she was admired beyond measure by the worthy working men and women who had seen her grow up at their side, and knew her true, kind heart. Whatever grudge they might be tempted to bear the other fine folk, whatever sly joke to crack at auld Tam's expense, at the very moment he was giving them so grand a ploy, they had nothing but admiration and tenderness for

Eppie in her bloom. The young girls in white muslin, with lockets and ear-rings hired from the village jeweller for the occasion, followed her about and watched her half the evening. Endless inquiries were made after Miss Eppie's grand young English 'laud;' he was reported a lord at least, and all the interest that could be spared from her was lavished on him. The couple far eclipsed Miss Drysdale and 'Captain Mackinnon' in the popular regard, though the last, as they were reckoned another pair of lovers, awoke their share of interest.

Auld Tam himself was in irreproachable black. Young Tam followed suit, defying the scornful eyes in the face of the vixen whom Dr. Peter had unwittingly reared. Yet Athole had the good taste not to wound the susceptibilities of her handmaid Jeannie by donning less festive apparel than was implied in a black tulle gown so quaintly and prettily trimmed by means of bands of silk, painted with tufts of buttercups, that if it was not a costly, it was certainly a becoming costume.

Sir Hugo would have come in a court suit if he had possessed one, and it would have given satisfaction in the right quarter. It was Guy Horsburgh who betrayed his friend into the solecism of arriving in the demi-toilette of a velvet morning-coat. But Tam Drysdale would have condoned any coat on 'Sir Hugie's' back, while young Eppie secretly thought him like a prince, and many of the rustic spectators were fully convinced that velvet coats were the specialty of English baronets and their friends.

There was a little difficulty as to who was to open the ball. It ought to have been Mrs. Drysdale and Sir Hugo, or Mrs. Drysdale with the oldest dyer in her husband's employment, followed by auld Tam either with Lady Semple or the rosy-cheeked granddaughter of his first bleacher. But neither of these arrangements met Tam's views. Besides, Mrs. Drysdale was timid about her steps, whether, on the one hand, she could accommodate them to those of 'Sir Hughie,' friendly as he had shown himself—to the extent of seeming to aspire to be her son-in-law—or whether, on the other, she could contrive to keep pace with Lowrie Leech, who was dead-lame.

There was some apprehension, amongst those interested in the proceedings of the couple, that auld Tam would open the ball himself, dancing with his wife; but if he had ever entertained the idea he thought better of it. He made a speech instead, and deputed the ceremony to a younger couple.

'My friends,' he said, with a flourish of his white, soft, but powerful hand, 'me and my wife are delighted to see you all here, and wish you a happy nicht. We are getting owre auld, as some of you may find yourselves, to lead either game or dance. When the band strikes up our auldest dochter will stand for her mither, and there's a gentleman here, whose name may be known to a wheen of you, that will do me the favour to lift her. Most of you aulder folk will mind that before I was maister here, Drysdale Haugh belonged to Mr. Mackinnon in richt of his wife. All here who mind were their servants aince on a day, and it is fit that the former maister and mistress of the place, who I make no doubt did their best for their folk in their time, should be remembered and represented on an occasion like this. Lieutenant Mackinnon, sir, I'll thank you to lead out my dochter and open the ball.'

The workpeople, who 'ruffed,' or beat with their feet, their applause, might accept Tam's speech in all sincerity, and regard this bringing forward of Guy Mackinnon's son as a generous, kindly deed, worthy of auld Tam; but his nearest and dearest trembled for him.

'Are there ony fivvers that take the head going about ?' the elder Eppie asked Dr. Peter, with a shiver; while the younger

Eppie turned to Sir Hugo, in their growing intimacy, with innocent perplexity: 'It is funny of father to make Mr. Mackinnon open the ball with Clary. I used to be sure that father did not like Mr. Mackinnon, and now to send him to dance with Clary!'

'It is because your father has compassion upon us young fellows,' said Sir Hugo promptly; 'and if he had known how I had set my heart on having this first dance which you are going to give to that urchin——'

'Little Willie Finlay, Sir Hugo,' Eppie interrupted. 'But I was bound to dance with Willie, for he is as deaf as a horn, though he is fond to dance, and he needs a partner that will help him through the figures. Besides, Clary and me have to dance with all our men in turn, which will take us half the night,' added Eppie a little mischievously. 'If you do not want to sit still for a couple of hours you had better let me introduce you to some of the girls who look so nice; to Willie's sister Mary, or to Sibbie Howden, or Camellia Duff.'

The couple opening the ball by commission were confounded—even Claribel was staggered. 'I ought to be well acquainted with my own father,' she said, with an uneasy laugh, 'but till lately I never suspected him either of dry humour or of diabolical malice.'

'Can he be giving in without a fight?' faltered Eneas. 'It has looked of late like his yielding without so much as a protest. He has not only been perfectly civil, he has been positively kind—asking me to come over with Semple, including me in all his invitations, and now distinguishing me like this. Does he care so much for you, Claribel, that he will swallow me and my poverty rather than cross you?'

Clary shook her head. 'My father has been a fighting man all his life, more than you have been. He has welcomed trials of strength and skill. Why should he shun a fight? He likes me, of course; he likes me so well as to let me have my own way, if I have set my heart upon it, because he is both reasonable and kind—I have always counted on that. But as to his weakly abetting me in the pursuit of an object which he does not believe to be for my good—remember he does not know you so well as I do—I suspect he would rather see me in my coffin. He must be giving us line, as you fishers say, and laughing at us, though I would not have expected it from him.'

Mrs. Drysdale had a second grievance in the course of the evening, which she took so much to heart that she could not keep it from Tam. It was a repetition of a former offence of which she had complained to him at the time; and she thought that if she could thoroughly rouse him to the aggravated nature of the redoubled injury, it might help to restore the balance of mind which he had so strangely lost.

'Tam,' she said, drawing her husband aside into a bower of laurels, ' I can stand this no longer. What do you think I have seen and heard? That gipsy of Dr. Peter's —that I should call her such a name!— taking off young Tam to his face, as if he were the smallest graith in the room, and putting him off from dancing till it is her pleasure; and the laddie standing it like a cawf. Oh! I could give him a dirl in the lug [box in the ear] mysel'; and I could bid her bide awa' from ony place I'm in, till she can behave herself as becomes a lassie like her, with due consideration for her betters. She's weel enough, though she's no bonnie; but she's not fit to be named in the same breath with my Tam, who is bewitched, I think.'

' Say you so!' answered auld Tam a little abruptly; then he pulled himself together, asserted he must see to it, and before she could stop him, crossed the room to where Athole Murray was sitting fluttering a fan—on which she had painted a yellowhammer in 'the de'il's livery' of sulphur-yellow and black, which corresponded with the black tulle and buttercups of her gown.

'Oh, mercy me! what have I done?' cried poor Mrs. Eppie, in dire dismay. 'If he speaks to her to quarrel her, though she weel deserves a hurry [scold], and it come to young Tam's ears, he'll neither be to haud nor bind. My laddie will never speak to his mither again. That lassie has driven him demented.'

But auld Tam addressed Athole with perfect politeness, even with an undercurrent of the special regard which he had always felt for her. 'I hope you're enjoying yoursel', Miss Murray, mem?'

'Very much, thank you, Mr. Drysdale,' replied Athole, with perhaps a suspicion of exaggerated emphasis, but with great goodwill, for, as she had said, she was fond of auld Tam — the two suited each other wonderfully. She brightened up at his approach, with a sense of security and confidence. He would not tease or misunderstand her. To encourage young Tam in his folly would be the last thing he would think of doing. At the same time he, auld Tam, could let his son take care of himself. Her father's friend would not sacrifice her to young Tam's dignity. He would be honest and friendly, giving her the credit of doing her best in a difficulty —how great and sore none save herself knew.

'I'm glad to hear you're happy,' Tam assured his guest with almost wistful earnestness. 'I want everybody to be happy the nicht. A treat means a rarity, and as one never kens whether it can be given twice by the same hand, I would fain do the thing thoroughly when I've the chance. I hope all the arrangements are to your mind?'

'Nothing could be better,' Athole said quickly—she was not quite so certain as she had been of her safety with auld Tam. His speech had already recalled to her mind that he had not been like himself lately. He was one of nature's gentlemen in the main, as she had always known— courteous and kind to his old friend's daughter; but he was more at this moment, he was pointedly, painfully deferential, as he had been at the picture sale. She did not like his manner. She could not tell what to make of it. 'I believe everybody is very happy,' she added vaguely; 'you may have the satisfaction of thinking that you have given a great deal of harmless pleasure to a number of people.'

'I have heard there are exceptions,' he said dubiously. 'I've a notion I've seen ae discontented face, and another that is petted, gin it be not peevish. Will you forgive an auld man—auld enough to be your father—your father's friend for that matter, for taking a liberty? What ails you at dancing with young Tam? If you're so happy yoursel', can you not spare a crumb to a poor beggar who has long been prigging [praying] for grace, this nicht aboon a' nichts, when everybody's heart is or should be as licht as his heels? Is it consistent with a gracious leddy's happiness to be glad when a gentleman suffers? or are you behaving on principle, Miss Murray, mem? I ken I've no richt to speer [ask]; but you and me have been gude friends—have we no?'

Athole stared and grew red and pale again in an instant. She flicked her dress with her fan bearing the bird that wears the de'il's livery. 'There is no poor beggar here,' she said sharply; 'you know that as well as I. If there were, it might be different. But, indeed, you have no right to say anything, though you are the owner of this place and the giver of this ball, though you employ me along with your workpeople. No,' she prevented a vehement protest, 'I do not mean for a moment that you have not been everything that is good and kind to me; but I hope I too know how to behave civilly—you see you have touched me on a sore point.' She gave a faint smile. 'Yet—well, I did not expect it from you. I wonder what Mrs. Drysdale would say? she knows better, after all. How would you judge of your wish that everybody should be happy—supposing I complied with it, and supposing you wasted a thought upon it to-morrow morning?' she ended bitterly.

For Athole had made the great mistake of imagining that auld Tam was so far left to himself as to desire she should gratify young Tam's inclinations for the moment, at the expense of her pride and consistency; that she should permit attentions of which nothing could come, in order to increase the hilarity of the evening, at least where one member of the party was concerned.

To her amazement and distress, in place of leaving her or losing his temper, or even begging her pardon, auld Tam began to plead passionately on behalf of his son. 'I've no richt to speak—less than none. I'm weel aware of it,' he said, in agitation which he could not conceal. 'Very likely he would be the first to blame me for advocating his cause—and why should he need an advocate with a leddy when he seeks her favours? He's a brawer man than ever his father was, and women like strapping chiels. He's been reared a gentleman, and he's nearer the real article than mony a lord. He is not saft or gay of speech—he's looking dour and dowff [stubborn and sad] enough at this minute when ilka other face is gay. But whose fault is that, I should like to know? It's ill for a lad to thole a lass's scorn, to be slichted when he has looted [bent], proud as he may be, to his knee. He's pairtner in a fine business, and he's making a grander business-man than I could ever have dreamt. His heart is in the richt place, and is as sound as a bell. What would you have mair?' demanded auld Tam, with rising indignation. 'Do you want his mither as well as his father to speak up for him? But is that like a reasonable leddy? My Eppie is as good a soul as ever breathed, but she's his mither, and so her ain bird is whitest among the craws; no other bird that he can choose will ever come nigh him for whiteness in her een. It's human nature, that; it's mither's nature. I thocht you would have understood and made allowance for 't, that it is useless to fecht against it. But I'll be bound she'll bear no spite, and come round as fast as ever woman came round, if no other man stand in the way—I've never heard tell of any other, and you could gar my Tam's heart lowp [leap] with a kind word or look, and take the wind when it blows in your barn-door.'

She got up and left him in the middle of his pleadings. She could stand no more of such raving. She found her father and clung to him, addressing half-a-dozen arguments to him in favour of going home early. As she stood awaiting his compliance with her request, she put it to him:

'Father, suppose a man does the very reverse of what you have been accustomed to see him do, and flies in the face of natural prejudices without the smallest reason, what would you think?'

'I can hardly tell, unless I were to know the man,' said canny Dr. Peter; 'but folk would have said lang syne that he was "fey."'

'I am sorry,' said Athole, in a low, grave tone.

'If you mean auld Tam, as I take it you do,' said her father, in the same key, 'so am I—sick and sorry. There's the devil to pay there, or I am much mistaken. I never thought to have witnessed the signs in this quarter. What is it? Over-trade, bad times, loss of credit, a heap of debt, an expensive style of living which cannot be altered without arousing suspicion? The result is the same — wild to get his daughters off his hands at a moment's notice, even though he can find no better protector for Clary than the penniless officer, Gavin Mackinnon's son, whom auld Tam was wont to despise. As for Sir Hugo, he would have been a big fish in the smoothest water, but one might have hoped that Tam Drysdale was above angling for it. Young Tam's looking put about, so that you need not have snapped at him, Athole. I suppose it is a bad custom you have fallen into. Well, since we can do no good, we had better keep out of the mess, for mess it will be.'

'I don't know what it all means,' said Athole, knitting her brows, 'unless that auld Tam's fey.'

Auld Tam brought forward Eneas Mackinnon a second time before the evening was over. When Tam's health was drunk, in returning thanks, he begged to couple them with the name of Lieutenant Mackinnon, the son of the former proprietor of Drysdale Haugh.

The toast sounded to many people, as possibly auld Tam intended it should, tantamount to announcing Claribel's engagement, and introducing young Mackinnon in the character of a member of the family.

Eneas muttered his gratitude in a couple

of words. Some among the audience thought it was a pity the response could not have been made by his future partner in life, who would have been quite equal to delivering a calm, well-bred, suitable little speech. She must coach her bridegroom in anticipation of the wedding breakfast.

CHAPTER XXXV.

SIR HUGO LAYS HIMSELF AND WILLOUGHBY COURT AT YOUNG EPPIE'S FEET.

GUY HORSBURGH threw up his last futile attempt to restrain Sir Hugo, to keep him back from a declaration of his sentiments before he had got time to cool, or before any aristocratic friend or batch of friends could interfere in his interests. Sir Hugo was of age; he was his own master, he could go his own way, as he showed every inclination to do. For the rest, Lady Willoughby must see to it, though Guy had first brought her son to Glasgow.

After all, the result was not so deplorable or so unexampled as it might have been. Sir Hugo was going to ally himself with trade; but so had earls and marquises before him. He was on the eve of proposing to marry one of the loveliest, sweetest girls in the West of Scotland, with a large fortune, if auld Tam cleared himself, as he certainly would, from the reverses of bad times. Sir Hugo might go farther and fare worse. Lady Willoughby might have an infinitely less satisfactory daughter-in-law thrust upon her. The whole Willoughby race might have reason to bless the day which had sent Sir Hugo to woo and win a fair and good Glasgow heiress.

Unquestionably Sir Hugo thought so. He was in the seventh heaven of young love—worthy as it was ardent, unlikely to be balked, and yet not so certain of its crowning success as to lack the stimulus of doubt and difficulty, the excitement of the chase. Would young Eppie Drysdale quit her country and her people, leave father and mother—though it was in the Bible that it could and should be done—for him, to go where he went, to dwell where he dwelt, to make his people, with their different ways, her people and her ways, till nothing but death should part her and him?

The gossips of St. Mungo had little doubt of the answer. They had lately wavered a little in their long-standing conviction of auld Tam's luck. He was known to be 'bitten' by more than one of the unfortunate traders who were succumbing on all sides to the ebb of the tide of trade. It was generally rumoured that his only son and elder daughter were about to make inferior matches. But the news of the probable engagement of Tam's younger daughter—a mere schoolgirl—to a grand young English baronet, with a 'Court' to take her to, quite restored the balance of her father's reputation for good fortune. Tam Drysdale knew what he was about, and he would keep at the top of the tree in spite of contradictions such as fell to the lot of the most prosperous of men. Young Eppie Drysdale 'Lady Willoughby of Willoughby Court!' Auld Tam might have been the Lord Provost and his daughter not fared so well.

That was the summer of life for some of the family at Drysdale Hall, though they were also the days in which little Eppie awoke to find herself a woman, to relinquish reluctantly her bright care-free girlhood, to realize her lot of merging her life in that of another, and being ready to sacrifice herself for him. If ever there were idyls enacted in modern times, that suit of Sir Hugo's, under the blatant auspices of trade, was one of them. He was so young, generous, and devoted; she was so simple and so sweet, so unworldly in her coming promotion, so unmoved by it, so genuinely humble, still so tenderly attached to all that she was nevertheless preparing to give up. Her nature, in place of being hardened and tarnished by the gain which came to her—as it must have come to every true woman in her circumstances—tempered by loss, was deepened and purified. All who had eyes to see stood still to look on and be moved by the domestic drama, when Eppie clung closer than ever to her father and mother, and spent upon them her most winsome wiles at the very time that she was singing 'My love she's but a lassie yet,' and 'What ails this heart o' mine?' every evening to Sir Hugo, hanging entranced upon her words. She did not so much as forget once poor deaf little Willie Finlay, or Beardie, or Whitebreeks, when the time came that Sir Hugo sought, with many excuses and apologies, almost to live at Drysdale Hall, when he was a miserably restless and discontented fellow if he was half a day out of the presence of its younger daughter in which he basked, when he haunted her and all connected with her like an exacting ghost. If he could not quite say of her that he

> 'Gat her down by yonder knowe,
> Smiling on a broomy knowe,
> Herding ae wee lamb and ewe,
> For her puir mammy;'

he could aver that he found her continually going on some errand of filial affection or human kindness. He called himself thrice blessed when she suffered him to meet her father with her, in her company to wait upon her mother, to do young Tam's bidding, to find something Clary wanted, to choose a picture-book for Willie Finlay, to take a warm jacket to Willie's consumptive cousin Maggie, to carry bones to Beardie and knobs of sugar to Whitebreeks.

When Sir Hugo thought of Eppie's relations to her homely father and mother, he contrasted them with what he had read, but declined manfully to believe, of 'girls of the period.' These daughters at ease were said to despise, in place of honouring, their fathers and mothers; to blush—not alone for the faults of the girls' progenitors, but for harmless peculiarities and rusticities which ought to have been sacred—might even have been dear—to the children of the perpetrators. Such girls were freely represented as rebelling against the lawful authority of their parents, and hating them with a hideous unnatural hatred. Sir Hugo was too good a fellow, too sensible and manly, to have much faith in the general existence of these unwomanly young women, and un-disciplined, undutiful heroines. But he recalled what he had seen of a very different order of girls living under the same roof with their fathers and mothers, yet practically apart from them, divided from them by a host of half-real, half-artificial obligations, trained to separate interests, occupations, and goals. Then his heart grew full, and he thanked God fervently that he had been shown another description of girl, another description of daughter —how true, how tender! one whom he could give to his own good mother, and know that he was rewarding her for all her care and affection where he was concerned, by bestowing on her—whether she knew it at first, or not, she would live to know it—the best of children.

It was as if the world had grown young

again this autumn at Drysdale Hall, and many who got a glimpse of scenes enacted in Paradise were touched by them, and became for the moment softened men and women. It was not only auld Tam and his Eppie who were thus affected—young Tam, with his dash of cynicism in his very philanthropy and his Radical views, did not accuse Sir Hugo of narrow arrogance and assumption, but was indulgent to him. Even young Tam was susceptible, shamefacedly, of a good deal of wondering half-humorous gratification at the idea of his sister, wild little Eppie, becoming Lady Willoughby. He secretly read up the English county history, which expatiated on the dignity and local benefactions of the Willoughbys, and on the antiquarian and architectural glories of the Lincolnshire Court. Insensibly Tam's bearing altered a little towards his young sister. It was not only softer, with a lurking, wistful affection in anticipation of losing her—a creature so deservedly dear to the family; it had a certain instinctive respect for the girl who was so soon to achieve matronly honours, who had made a slave of a fellow with wit and independence in his own line, like Sir Hugo, so that he stooped from his class and defied their censure, in seeking a city girl for the future mistress of his home.

And all the time she to whom this subtle tribute was paid thought hardly at all, unless it were with fear and trembling, of rank such as Sir Hugo owned, and social position like that to which he would raise her.

Claribel had foreseen young Eppie's conquest from the beginning, and accepted it fully. Now, in the engrossment of her own very different engagement to Eneas Mackinnon, tacitly allowed by her father, without a word spoken, Clary not only welcomed her sister's higher fortunes—she found leisure and energy to try to prepare Eppie for them. It was not by polishing her manners, for, since these had their share in captivating Sir Hugo, Clary wisely left off attempting to improve upon them, deciding that they had their charm for ancient gentility. It was in gently opening Eppie's eyes to what the future held for her, and accustoming her to the change which awaited her.

Claribel had taken great pleasure in presiding over Eppie's toilet lately, and in insisting that her particular style and taste should have every advantage which high art and accomplished modistes could give them.

'I don't wish you to be anything save yourself, Eppie dear,' said Clary. 'I do not know that you could be greatly improved, and I am certain I should never be forgiven if I destroyed your identity. Somebody's indignation would pursue me for the rest of my days. But there are various kinds of simplicity, and you ought to deal in the most perfect kind, which unites nature and art. You are bound to use the allowance that my father makes to each of us, which, as you have just grown up, you have entered upon so lately, you little chit. But to use it as the giver intended is not to spend the greater part of it in presents to him and my mother, which you know they do not require, though they may be pleased by your thinking of them in that way, and in gifts to servants and children and poor people. You ought to learn to have your dress, your *tout ensemble*, according to your station, or harm will come of it. That reminds me, when I came out I got my choice of any set of jewels short of diamonds, like mother's, that I preferred, and I took corals. What will you have? Not topazes—they are pink, but you must not be all pink. I should have opals if I were you, Eppie; they suit any colour, and they would not be too much for you.'

'Oh! don't speak about it, Clary,' cried Eppie, half-radiant, half-shrinking. 'I think father has a good deal to do with his money this year. I am sure he looks duller than he used to look. I can scarcely ever get him to make fun and laugh, as I once could I heard Tam and Dr. Peter speaking of bad trade.'

'What has a baby like you to do with bad trade?' demanded Claribel incredulously. 'Do you think what we spend makes any difference to our father? What the whole house spends is a drop in the ocean of his business outlay. It would be another thing if one of us married a poor man, a man with a small settled income, which could never become much larger—like an officer's pay,' added Clary, with a meaning smile; 'then that foolish woman must cut her gown according to her cloth.'

'And wouldn't she be happy to do it if it were for her man's sake!' cried Eppie, blushing very red and taking Clary aback by a sudden hug, which hid Eppie's blushes.

'Oh, my gown, Eppie!' protested Clary.

'What about your gown?' replied Eppie recklessly, returning to the main point. 'Oh,

I like you for it, Clary; and I am so glad to see that father is beginning to take to the Lieutenant.'

'Is he? I am not sure,' said Claribel, with unwonted indecision. 'My father has puzzled me lately. All the same, child, I am very thankful that you are not going to follow my example. One disinterested goose is enough in a family. I did not mean to be that goose, but Fate and Eneas Mackinnon have been too strong for me. Fancy poor dear Eneas being too strong for anybody! But there are those who overcome by lack of strength—if passive endurance is lack of strength. I am strong enough in the common, vulgar way, for both: I believe I have been wasted in the family for want of somebody to take care of, you are all so well off and independent. I first found my mission when the old Miss Mackinnons suffered me to look after them. But don't let us forget what we are talking about— you must have your opals, Eppie.'

'They are things that should belong to a

grand lady. It would fike me to take care of them.'

'But you are going to be a grand lady, little woman; and if you are not able to keep opals, what are you to do with diamonds? I have no doubt old Lady Willoughby has family diamonds which will pass to her son's wife.'

'She is not old,' cried Eppie, staunch as ever in maintaining the earthly immortality of her seniors. 'He says he remembers her looking so young and pretty, in spite of her widow's cap. She was not twenty-three when his father died,' explained Eppie shyly and softly. 'She will wear her diamonds as long as she lives—who has such a good right? who would take them from her?—and she will leave them to whom she likes. I'm sure he would say so. But oh, it is all nonsense!' broke off Eppie, in trepidation. 'I wish you would not speak about it, Clary. He has never speered me; and do you think I could bear to go away from father and mother and all of you at Drysdale Hall, where I've been so happy ? It would just kill me.'

'You would come alive again and live for him,' said Claribel, with smiling faith. 'He has not asked you in so many words to be his wife. Perhaps as you are so young, though he is young himself, he may choose to put the question to my father first. But I know he has talked to you by the hour of his home, and how you would like it, and what you would do there. As he is a gentleman and not an adventurer, true and not false, you will have it in your power to be the mistress of Willoughby Court, and you will not send him away— such a nice fellow as he is—disconsolate. I wonder if you will condescend to receive a poor officer and his wife some day at your fine place, Eppie ?'

The suggestion was too much for Eppie in the highly-wrought state of her feelings. What was she, that she should ever live to patronize Clary and the Lieutenant ? The bare idea smote her with affront and distress, so that she burst into hysterical tears, and had to be coaxed and scolded back into composure.

Auld Tam and his Eppie were stirred to the very depths of their natures, when the destiny of their darling was wrought out before their eyes. Many a time Mrs. Drysdale, even while her motherly eyes glistened with pride and joy, withdrew to 'greet' (weep) in secret over the relinquishment of her child. To think that little Eppie, who had always been as fondly faithful to her earliest ties as when she was a toddling child, who had never been three months absent from home, or a week away from her father and mother since she was born, should

'Aye be awa','

and in the very greatness of her marriage parted from them by barriers to which the Cheviots and the Tweed were nothing; to remember that if she had waited for some years, and married in an ordinary fashion a moderately thriving manufacturer or merchant in her father's circle, she might have been settled near Drysdale Hall—she might have seen her whole family two or three times a week as a matter of course— these considerations ought to have been a cure for ambition. But the mother was equal to the offering up of her very heart's blood for the object of her love. Being sure of 'Sir Hughie,' as Mrs. Drysdale believed herself, that he was a fine lad who would be good to young Eppie, the mother would not stand as an obstacle in the daughter's path. She would be ready when the time came to do more than cut off a right hand and pluck out a right eye. So that little Eppie might be a grand lady, loved and honoured in a higher sphere, then big Eppie, who had borne her and delighted in her young charms, would be content with the crumbs which fell from the rich man's table, with passing glimpses of her bairn, and more or less distant reports of her dignity and happiness.

Auld Tam was not so sure either of his

child or of himself. Young Eppie would be safe, though there should be a storm and downfall—that was one good thing which had tempted him. But could he endure to think that she would go where she might be looked down on, instead of made much of—scorned in place of cherished? Her little rustic ways, with love lying at their root, though 'Sir Hugie' had not minded them, or had gone so far as to be captivated by them, for a change, in these his red-hot love days, might look different in his eyes when the ways had lost their novelty, and marriage had cooled his passion and restored his judgment. Trifles like these sometimes made mischief between man and wife.

Tam Drysdale could ill stand the thought of his innocent, loving lassie being mortified and 'lichtlied' (slighted). He would come bound that she would never 'lichtly' her mother and him in her turn—it was not in her constant, gentle heart. But she might be taught to 'think shame' for those who had been first with her—whom, until now, in her guilelessness and goodness, she had well-nigh worshipped.

That was a prospect which auld Tam had difficulty in facing. He did not doubt 'Sir Hugie' in so far as that he meant well and was an honourable and kindly-disposed young gentleman. But Tam Drysdale had heard that like should mate with like, and he could not pretend to say that his bairn —bonnie and dear as she was to him— ought to be reckoned a fit match for a real gentleman—a titled gentleman of solid acres and long descent. And if in the time to come 'Sir Hugie' should be further disappointed in what he might conceive he had a right to expect—should have reason to say that he had not been candidly and honestly dealt with—could auld Tam be certain that the disappointment and the offence would not be visited on a blameless victim? The retaliation might not be open, but indirect and half unconscious, partly concealed from the very person who was guilty of the meanness of using such weapons, so as to be less easy to challenge and denounce ; but the undeserved punishment would fall on the tender heart, already writhing under a sense of the failure of those it had once exalted.

To Tam's other heavy troubles was added yet this one more grave perplexity, whether in promoting young Eppie's great marriage he was not really wronging her, his pet lamb, worst of all, and cruelly risking her best chance of happiness.

When all else was said, a quivering note of interrogation was added to what went before—Had the business not gone too far to be stopped ? Was it possible for him still to draw back ? Poor auld Tam! he was pulled two ways and torn in different directions, till he hovered on the verge of distraction.

Little wonder that Tam Drysdale, towards the end of Sir Hugo's courtship, looked, as often as not, heavy and displeased on what was evidently approaching its legitimate conclusion. He caused the by-standers to exclaim in a high key among themselves—What would the man be at? —was there no end to his ambition? Did he seek dukes for his daughters? or was it a mere feint of indifference and scanty approval, unworthy of auld Tam's character for sincerity?

CHAPTER XXXVI.

THE SEAL TO SIR HUGO'S SUIT.

The prettiest episode of Sir Hugo's wooing occurred when Lady Semple suddenly struck out the bright idea of bringing down Lady Willoughby to pay her a visit and judge for herself, when it was too late, of her son's choice.

Far from Sir Hugo's offering any objection—as if he were ashamed of what he was about, or had the slightest conception that his feelings might undergo a change, or that anybody, even his mother, to whom he was so strongly attached, had the smallest right to interfere with him in his choice of a wife—he was charmed with the opportunity of introducing the Drysdales, especially Eppie, to Lady Willoughby; and at the same time, though he was his own master, and was not very down-hearted about winning the day, he caught at the chance of securing his mother's potent voice on the side of his suit.

Sir Hugo had so talked himself into the belief of the transcendent merits of the merchant princes of St. Mungo's, he had so swallowed wholesale the peculiarities of the Drysdale household, and then, with his strong young mental and moral digestion, dismissed them without any great effort, that he had for the moment ceased to be conscious of their existence. He was only aware of a long list of commercial virtues, and that young Eppie was the loveliest, most artless, most divine of mortal maidens.

Sir Hugo met his mother unembarrassed and without apprehension—rather triumphant in having done so well by himself and her. She was full of pain at the thought of losing her son so soon, as it seemed to her; of doubt of his youthful wisdom in this direction, when love—above all, a boy's love—was notoriously blind; of rising repulsion—good as she was—at the trading middle-class into which he had strayed. He was only eager to escort her to Drysdale Hall, and to present her, as his best credentials, to his friends. To her mingled indignation, relief, and reluctant amusement, she found her boy was making his own of this visit of hers, which had been paid with another intention. In spite of Lady Semple's flowing accounts of the unobjectionable, indeed the very delightful, young Glasgow heiress who had happily captivated Sir Hugo, Lady Willoughby was come down on a mission of anxious inspection, agitated inquiry, and, if need were, in her son's interests, grieved but determined opposition—powerless as she was to hinder his will—with the hope, at least, of holding him back for a moment from wrecking his life for a young man's idle fancy. And here was he marshalling her as his complacent mother who was lending her countenance to his infatuation!

Lady Willoughby became confused and nervous with the turn matters had taken, but Sir Hugo offered an unmoved countenance. Auld Tam swaggered, though not so briskly as of old, over his possessions. Mrs. Drysdale, in the height of her timidity and her devotion to her child—the quality which of all things would have touched the visitor, had she been capable of measuring the large amount of fellow-feeling between the mistress of the house and herself—was at once unduly fine and unduly humble, and blundered hopelessly in her small affectations. It was all lost on the couple's future son-in-law, who smiled with cheerful unconcern, as if he knew better, as if everything were right in the main. Neither young Tam nor Claribel was of any use as interpreter and smoother-down of grievances, though Lady Willoughby saw at a glance that they were, in the language of her class, 'civilized' like other people.

Lady Semple, who had created the imbroglio, struck in energetically, and talked on every subject under the sun, to no purpose.

It was, as it should have been, young Eppie—who was not exactly civilized, and not like other girls of her age whom Lady Willoughby had known—that, without intending it, came to the rescue, and prevented the interview from proving an utter failure—nay, what was worse, an irretrievable disaster. Yet, strange to say, Eppie had never shown herself so refractory, so unmanageable. She was coy to the verge of absurdity and provocation of the most indulgent of her friends. Eppie declined absolutely to be trotted out by Lady Semple. The girls shrank away from the perfectly gentle Lady Willoughby, who was nearly as much put out, and a great deal sorer in heart than anybody else present, though her years and her good breeding had taught her to control herself and put the best face on a difficulty. Even in her unwillingness to come forward and distinguish Eppie, her ladyship was yet desirous of being quite courteous, if possible gracious, to everybody. She might be there to forbid the banns, but it would be done in the most reasonable, forbearing manner.

But little Eppie looked at Lady Willoughby, of whom the girl had spoken reverently and tenderly, as if the lady was an aristocratic tyrant of the old régime and the first water, come to annihilate the maiden for beguiling her son.

'It was all his doing,' Eppie, standing at bay, kept saying to herself. 'I would never have so much as looked at him—he who might have had Clary or anybody; but he sought me out as if he liked me best, and how could I withstand him?'

All the same she withstood Lady Willoughby, who was like her son. Eppie turned her back upon her ladyship unmistakably; she would not be drawn forward, but kept at a distance from the visitor, and left other people to entertain her.

Eppie answered her interrogator in monosyllables when Lady Willoughby forced herself to address the little rustic beauty who had won her son. Eppie did not so much as care that Sir Hugo began to look vexed. She was unjust for the moment, but it was an innocent, disinterested injustice. Let him take away his mother and leave Eppie to hers, for with a sudden revulsion Eppie turned and clung to her mother, held by her skirts, as it were, and would not be taken away from her.

It was this very attitude of rebellion and defiance, this simple clinging to the 'common woman,' her mother, and ignoring the lady, Sir Hugo's mother, together with Eppie's winsome, youthful loveliness, which broke down Lady Willoughby's defences. It was the old story of 'My boy Tammy' over again, of the true woman who knew by unerring instinct that her son could not be wrong in loving the 'young thing' whose heart was so full of her 'mammy,' and by an answering sweet and noble impulse ratified his choice.

Lady Willoughby commenced, not so much to unbend — for she was always modest and meek—as to warm. She took no further notice of young Eppie, but she smiled a wonderfully frank, kind smile upon mother Eppie and auld Tam. She began to speak pleasantly, and in the most friendly manner, of her son as of a person in whom they too were interested. She looked around her with observant eyes, and took notice of all the things he had written about and described to her, delicately indicating that, though he might, if he would, take the most important step in life without her consent, he had not taken it without her knowledge—he had kept no secrets from his mother. She ended by making herself at home during her short stay, and manifesting a sincere and flattering desire to be better acquainted in the future with everything and everybody at Drysdale Hall, for at present she was merely passing a day with the Semples at Semple Barns on her way to another friend's country-house—as it happened, the home of the Honourable Lilias, who held Dick Semple in her chains.

Then young Eppie stole from her mother's side and went into the conservatory, still refusing Sir Hugo's attendance and assistance. She gathered with her own hands, daring and defying the ogre of a head-gardener, some of the most choice flowers, and arranged them as only she and her mother knew how. Eppie came back when Lady Willoughby's foot was already on the step of the Semple Barns carriage, followed her and made the peace-offering mutely, with changing colour and untutored grace.

Lady Willoughby turned as lightly as if she had been only half her age, accepted the flowers, and equally without a word, kissed and smiled on the giver. That kiss and that smile were the sign of free forgiveness, Lady Willoughby's seal to her son's suit which neither Sir Hugo's wife nor Sir Hugo's mother were ever likely to forget.

'She will do, Hugo,' his mother confessed to him in private. 'She would have been a perfect love of a girl, whether she had been a princess or a peasant. I do not know that I could have wished one better or half so good for you, perhaps. But oh, my dear boy! it was running a terrible risk for you to go out of your rank, and lose your heart without so much as thinking what you were about. And I doubt there will be difficulties; you will have to be very patient, very generous, very prudent, Hugo. I am afraid you do not know yet what you are doing. Though she were the sweetest, dearest girl in the world, when there is anything like a *mésalliance*, there is a great deal to bear.'

'Nonsense, mother. These merchant princes look down upon us poor "landed gentry," as they call us. They don't need to covet matches with us. Besides, Mr.

and Mrs. Drysdale are excellent people, you must see that; and I don't care a rap for things,' the young man went on in one of his high flights, speaking rather incoherently. 'I believe I am thick-skinned. The risk has been well repaid, and, if you are satisfied, it is all right; that is, if she will have me, if she will make up her mind to exchange Drysdale Hall for Willoughby Court.'

Lady Willoughby did not answer. She had made great concessions, but she would indeed have been a wonderful woman if, with her nurture, she could have realized that to some people, and those not the worst in the world, Drysdale Hall in its over-blown splendour might have attractions superior to Willoughby Court with its fine flavour of old gentility.

After all, when Sir Hugo made his formal proposal, and asked Eppie's hand from her father, the young man was astonished and disappointed by auld Tam's returning him a doubtful, evasive answer.

Tam Drysdale expressed himself as much obliged, he ought to say honoured, by 'Sir Hugie's' offer. He was perfectly aware of the compliment which had been paid to his daughter; but there was time enough to think of her marriage; she was very young. He could not answer 'Sir Hugie' positively at that moment, or indeed for some time to come—not even after Eppie's father should have ascertained her feelings on the subject.

All a lover's eloquence and impatience were wasted in vain, in spite of the fact that Sir Hugo had been accustomed to find himself treated as a person of consequence all his life. Auld Tam would not stir from his position. He was much obliged and highly honoured, etc., etc. He did not desire to be ungracious or rude, but he could not give an absolute answer at a moment's notice. He must have time to think over matters. Sir Hugo must wait. If little Eppie were not worth waiting for, then the young gentleman had better let her alone and go his way. 'Dod!' he might be thankful that he got no worse answer; he himself had been forced to speer twice at auld Mercer, who knew him a hantle better than he knew 'Sir Hugie,' before he got his Eppie.

Sir Hugo might have replied that the circumstances were different, and that something more was due to him. But he refrained. He certainly thought young Eppie worth waiting for, and after the first shock of mortified pride and baffled ardour was surmounted, the ingenuous nature and excellent temper of the young man came out in the good grace with which he submitted to the uncalled-for period of uncertainty and probation to which he was sentenced. Nobody could see any reason for the trial, but Sir Hugo came off so far the victor by cleverly making stock of auld Tam's hesitation. Sir Hugo managed not only to secure the sympathy and support of the bride and all the other members of her family, but to prove to his mother and the connections of his house acquainted with the affair, the truth of his assertion of the disinterestedness and superiority of the merchant princes, and how guiltless they were in the person of Mr. Drysdale of Drysdale Hall of any anxiety to bestow a daughter on Sir Hugo Willoughby.

It was auld Tam's own household that were most aggrieved by his conduct.

'What does my father mean?' demanded young Tam, with a fellow-feeling for his brother bachelor in the ordeal he was made to pass through. 'He ought not to have suffered Sir Hugo to come so much here, if my father intended to object at the last moment.'

'He will get Eppie and all of us talked about,' complained Claribel. 'People will not understand. They will suppose Sir Hugo has drawn back, or that there is some trouble with the settlements.'

'Oh, does father not like him? What fault can father find with him? I'm sure he likes father,' poor Eppie pled piteously with her mother, till what Mrs. Drysdale called her 'corruption,' her unregenerate nature, was roused to remonstrate strongly in her turn with her husband.

'Would you mar your bairn's credit and happiness, Tam Drysdale, for a freit [fancy] at this time of the day?' Nobody feels more keenly than me that she is going out from us, that we are giving her up to the fine lad. But they're a braw young couple. Eppie will be my leddy, and what for no? If Providence has willed her promotion, my bit lassie is worthy to wear a crown, like Queen Esther in the Auld Testament. We've no earthly title to prevent it. What's come ower you that you dinna see that? What makes you sae thrawn [cross], lad?'

But neither did auld Tam yield to the wife of his bosom. He had always the same answer to give—time enough. He must think. He would give his consent, or it might be his denial, when it was fitting. If Sir Hugie could not stay—let him go.

CHAPTER XXXVII.

A CHARMED SAIL.

In the middle of auld Tam's perversity, he suddenly announced that he would take a holiday sail. He had never set up a yacht of his own, neither had young Tam adopted that refuge and glory of a maritime people, especially of the young swells of the mercantile world of the West of Scotland. But there were various friends' yachts at auld Tam's disposal the moment he signified his intention. Neither was company likely to fail him; but here he was as arbitrary as he had been lately in other matters. He would have nobody with him save the two Eppies. He would not allow the presence of young Tam, saying that he might be wanted at the office and works in his father's absence. But neither would Tam have Clary with him, though she was an experienced and excellent yachtswoman; she should stay at home and keep house while her mother was away; and he actually scouted the suggestion of the attendance of Sir Hugo, who had nothing else to do, would have liked nothing in the world better, and made humble overtures to be allowed to join the party. The planner of the expedition desired a rest—complete, however short—from the toils of business, and, for that matter, of hospitality; and to procure this he must have none except the two members of his family whom he had chosen—his wife and his younger daughter —to sail with him.

The drawbacks were that neither of the Eppies were good sailors, that both had a most unaffected dislike to spending days and nights at sea, and that though the weather was remarkably fine for the season, the month of October had been reached, with its lengthening nights, shortening days, chill, frosty air, and sudden gales, striking terror into the hearts of landswomen.

But the two women on whom auld Tam had pitched to bear him company would never fail their lord and master. Had it been Styx and not Clyde he had fixed on for his watery highway, and had Charon and not an honest man from Largs been the steersman of the vessel, the two Eppies would have gone down as devotedly and almost as intrepidly, with a certain fond pride that auld Tam should have elected them for the partners of his voyage. It did not signify that their faces were pale —the elder Eppie's from sheer quaking before an anticipated experience so foreign and unpalatable to her, and with the thought of the home and children she might never see again, if auld Tam, his company and crew, went to the bottom, in this unchancy autumn trip on which he had set his heart in a strange, almost an uncanny manner. As for the younger Eppie, her sweet colour was gone, because her tender heart was wrung by the injustice and injury done to her lover, while yet she did not dream of resisting her father—loyal still to auld Tam in the worst of his caprices.

The sail was not to be very prolonged or to involve further risk than could not be avoided in a change of weather with the squally gusts concentrated in the passes between the mountains, which sometimes lend a peculiar peril to such coast-sailing. For auld Tam meant merely to run up one or other of the arms of the sea with which all the dwellers in the region are familiar, to lie to in the shadow of the everlasting hills each night, and resume his course on the following morning.

There was no sign of any fall of the barometer or chopping of the wind, which was in fact too light, with no more than a harmless ripple on the water, when the little freight started from the pier at

Greenock, to which the carriage and steamboat had transported them, leaving behind a disconsolate group of persons, who had insisted on accompanying their friends so far, looking wistfully after them. The least affected of the group were Claribel and Eneas Mackinnon, who had ventured unrebuked, unless by his own unaccounted-for success, to make himself one of the family. They were neither of them overburdened with imagination, and they had enough of business of their own on their hands to occupy them. He contented himself with observing on the cut of the yacht and calculating the rate of her speed; and Clary's moan was summed up in declaring that really her mother and Eppie had no excuse for being ill. Then the couple dropped the subject for others more interesting to them, as they moved away, he sauntering by her side, in the ᴜ ' ble style of their progress through

ng Tam muttered discontentedly,

'I cannot tell what has come over my father —a yacht trip in October, and my mother and Eppie frightened out of their wits if the sails fill or the deck inclines a quarter of an inch.'

Sir Hugo said nothing. He was haunted with the vision of an old picture he had seen abroad of the Virgin Mary, her mother St. Anne, and St. Joseph, sailing away on a shoreless sea, and with the echo of the refrain of one of young Eppie's saddest songs—

> 'Ochone! for fair Helen, ochone!
> Ochone! for the flower of Strathco:
> In the deep, deep sea,
> In the saut, saut bree,
> Lord Reoch, thy Helen lies low!'

Sir Hugo had to put the greatest force upon himself to resist rushing off, securing another yacht, and following in the wake of the Drysdales. He had just enough judgment left to recognise that no measure would so offend and outrage auld Tam as the invasion of his privacy to which the young man was tempted.

In reality no such tremendous calamity as the shipwreck or foundering of the yacht threatened auld Tam and his faithful womankind. The little vessel was as good and serviceable as any Clyde-built craft which has an honourable reputation. The skipper and crew were picked men of their class, to be depended upon in all circumstances. The weather continued uninterruptedly fine, so as to soothe the excitable feelings even of the two Eppies.

'Oh, it is bonnie, mother; I never knew it would be so bonnie!' said young Eppie, standing, without tottering, in her dark serge costume, with only her cheeks, rosy once more, to relieve it, as she watched the blue water over which the yacht rode lightly, and the autumn-tinted hills and woods of the shore. 'If it is all like this, I don't think we'll be feared, and it will be a fine change for father from the Haugh and Glasgow.'

'Bairn, I never saw sic weather in October,' said her mother, still inclined to be awed, if not appalled. 'It is just a ferlie [marvel]. Eh! how gude it will be for the petawties diggin' and pittin'. If your father had only ta'en a thocht of driving ower to my auld hame—though it is in the hands of strangers now—and of bidin' a day or twa, to watch the farm folk at their wark, or to fish in the burn, I could have baked scones sic as he was fond o' lang syne to give him an appetite. But, as you say, if the water is nae waur than this, it will be a fine change, and it may do him a heap of gude; poor chield, he has been forfochten [over-worked], as he kens best, of late!'

Auld Tam did not seem to reap immediate advantage from the variety he had sought. He was still engrossed and oppressed, and paced up and down, taking little notice of his wife and daughter. But as the hours wore on, and the breeze—though it was no more than a summer breeze—blew fresher, the wavelets curled with a whiter crest, and the thickly-populated banks gave place to lonelier, wilder regions, where the woods of Finnart embowered the hamlet of Ardentinny, and higher and higher rose the heathery hills, showing nothing but sheep-tracks and the furrows worn by winter torrents, till the great mass of the Cobbler loomed dark against the early sunset, auld Tam shook himself up, as if the wind and the water were blowing away the cobwebs from his brain. He took note of each well-known landmark, and pointed it out carefully to his companions—not so familiar with the scene. He told them the stories he had heard in his boyhood—how the Danes had landed there; and here the clan Macfarlane had shouted their slogan 'Lochsloy! Lochsloy!' when they started to levy blackmail and plunder and murder whoever resisted them. He cheered the Eppies with prophecies of the settled nature of the weather—more to be depended on than in early summer—which would last their trip. He foretold how quietly the yacht would lie off Arrochar till morning broke. He incited the ladies to have an informal scrambling meal—a sort of tea, dinner, and supper in one—of roast fowl and cold round, ham and tongue, partridges, cheese, and oysters, with bitter beer, claret and Glenlivat, tea and coffee, toast and cake, grapes and melons, eaten and drunk on deck. Tam Drysdale waited on his wife and daughter in spite of their remonstrances, as if he were proud to be their servant; and he did not forget the shy, independent sailors who drew off from witnessing the feast, and could only be induced by an instantly established freemasonry of jokes and grins between auld Tam and the crew, and gentle solicitations from the two gentlewomen of whom the men were taking care, to accept a share of the good things lavishly provided for the occasion.

Auld Tam was himself again, and the two Eppies could not help being glad, though night was falling, and though they had still the fearful experience before them of descending to their cabin and going to bed rocked on the bosom of the deep. In the meantime the moon and star light shone white over Arrochar, causing the mountains to throw blacker shadows, and the twinkling lamps of the village to look red and yellow, and the water between to glisten with a trembling radiance. The stillness, now that the yacht had stopped sailing, acquired something of mystery, like everything else in the unwonted surroundings. It was a clear, cold night, frosty indeed, but there was no fog, and the air was so pure and rare that it was not unpleasant to meet it, enveloped in the multitude of 'haps'—cloaks and plaids, hoods and clouds—with which Mrs. Drysdale had taken care to come provided. The women stayed on deck, impressed, as these simple souls had not expected to be, by the new world around them.

The elder Eppie kept close to her Tam, felt as if they were one again, and was wonderfully content to sit by him while he smoked in silence, or occasionally uttered a brief word of admiration, for auld Tam was a great admirer of nature in an old-fashioned, solemnized style.

The younger Eppie drew away by herself. She sat a little behind the mast, and looked up with great innocent eyes at the lustrous moon, asking herself if *he* were looking at it as she was, and knowing that he must, for she was sure that he was watching every turn of the weathercock and every cloud in the sky till she was safe on land again. She wished he were there, but she felt they would not be long apart, for her father must relent, and then Sir Hugo would not grudge her for these few days to him. And oh! she would try to be good to her man, as she tried to be good to her father and mother, and God would bless them and take care of them for evermore. As little Eppie gazed across the moonlit waters, a strange transformation took place. She ceased to see the dim mountains looming around her, the dark loch at her feet, the planks and ropes of the yacht close at hand. She beheld, what her bodily eyes had never rested upon, but what she had heard often described with love's eloquence. She saw the rich foliage of a double row of spreading lime trees in a green park, the low square tower of a Norman church rising above the mossy park-wall on one side, and a red house, all mullioned windows and peaked gables, with flower-beds and an ancient fountain and sundial on a terrace. And she knew it was his English home on which the same moon was shining as it might shine when the home was hers also, when she had quitted Scotland and the west, and he was teaching her to be such a lady as his mother was. Lady Willoughby was grander in her soft unconscious dignity than stately Clary or restless Lady Semple. Yet Lady Willoughby had taken Eppie's flowers and stooped and kissed her, and, Eppie knew, had received her, for Lady Willoughby's son's sake, into a second mother's heart, true and tender as Eppie's own mother's. Had the girl not reason to be grateful?

The morning rose with a more silvery haze than if the season had been summer, though during the night that had passed the frost had laid fiery fingers on what was left of the heather, on the leaves of the sapling oaks and the light tresses of the birk-trees—only the dark-green firs, like the hills above them, defied cold, heat, storm, sunshine.

The hours of sleep might have been dreamful and restless, spent so far from home, where everything was so out of gear, as even the most luxurious yacht's cabin appeared to the dwellers in Drysdale Hall; but nothing save refreshment could come from the caller air, the sparkling water, the mist like curdled milk, or flakes of wool drawn back and up into the highest recesses of the hills. Mrs. Eppie had another and a lower source of happiness by which maiden Eppie was not altogether unmoved—not only were they miraculously escaping the pandemonium of sea-sickness which they had braved like two heroines for the love of auld Tam, half a day and a night of the pilgrimage were gone, and they were so much nearer to home and Sir Hugo.

The opening into another loch with an island and a ruined castle was passed, and the Kyles between Bute and Cowal were entered. The October sun streamed down mellow, not wan as yet, on crags and knolls, grey pinnacles, ferny dells and bickering burns, on Colintraive and Tighnabruaich, deserted by their summer visitors, left to hardy fishers and herdsmen. Ardlamont Point was turned and Kilbrandon Sound reached, leaving Tarbet with its tower, and Ardrishaig with its early steamboat behind. Lochfyne presented a noble land-locked water, bearing in the season fleets of brown herring-boats swaying with the tide. On its shores, glens, valleys, and mountains succeeded each other. Here was the glen of the Leakan; yonder flashed the waters of the Uray and the Shira; that peaked hill was Dunaquoich, and in its shelter rose the castle of M'Callummore.

Auld Tam was peaceful as the weather, pleased as his companions. He coaxed the two Eppies into a small boat, to undergo the penance of being rowed up a minor water to the shore where the channel was narrowest; and the bank he chose offered nothing but shelving rock, rough grass, bracken and blackberries, curlews and plovers with their shrill, ear-piercing cries. Perhaps the place was seen more in character when autumn was beginning to add to the natural desolation of the scenery, than in spring or summer.

Tam Drysdale rewarded his companions for their submission to his fancies by letting them sit down and look at sea and sky, all bright and glad in contrast to the earth, and at the yacht reflected in the blue water; or to scramble till even the youngest scrambler's light feet were tired.

The solitude and the stillness sank into minds unaccustomed but not irresponsive to such influences, and first thrilled the guileless hearts through and through, and then calmed their throbbing pulses.

As young Eppie sought to pluck the last red ling, singed by the nightly pinches of frost, over which the bees, safe in their binks until the summer returned, had ceased to hover, with the lingering tufts of thrift or sea-pink whitening under the salt spray by the water's edge, she kept humming—

> 'Lowland lassie, will you go
> Whaur the hills are clad wi' snow;
> Whaur, beyond yon icy steep,
> The Highland shepherd tends his sheep?'

and pointed exultingly to the farthest-away mountain which had white streaks across its bald front. But if she had known it, these signs which she took to be the harbingers of approaching winter had survived all the summer sunshine, and were no more like the glorious but ghastly livery of the death of the year than the little streamlet issuing from the well-eye is like the great river hurrying to the edge of the precipice and leaping fiercely to destruction before it loses itself in the islandless sea.

'Everything looks auld, auld, and yet as fresh as on the day of creation,' said the elder Eppie, while the three figures, like the three corbies to which auld Tam compared them, perched themselves on some stones and appeared the only moving, breathing objects in the landscape. 'Tam, it's like being alane in the presence of ane's Maker.'

'Yet the boat is in sicht and fishing-cobles forbye, and the next minute a steamer full of the world's racket may come tearing through the water, leaving a long wreath of black smoke filing [defiling] the blue lift [air]. There are far loner spots than this within a day's sail, if it had been fit to venture there with timorous women so far on in the year. But this may serve,' said Tam, half-absently and with a sigh—'this taste of the world as God made it. What do you think, Eppie, woman? It's grand in its very nakedness, and on few lines, like a' His wark—nothing weak or ower saft and fine and dilittanty about it. It mak's us ashamed of the feck [most] of our wark. What do you think? We could strip ourselves of our warks, as the preachers call them, in His sicht, and lay them down and leave them without breaking our hearts. What do you think?' he kept repeating eagerly.

'You're richt, Tam, no doubt,' said his wife gently, but with only the most superficial guess at his meaning. 'We brocht naething into the world, and we'll tak' naething out—that's plain. And all our bravery that we set sic store on is no more than bairns' toys that the bairns are brodent [keen] on for a day and forget the next.'

'Men's praise amang the lave,' chimed in Tam.

'Ay, men's praise or blame will fa' dead where there are nae lugs [ears] greedy to kep it. But are you no weel, Tam, my man,' asked Eppie anxiously, 'that you speak in so serious a strain?'

'Oh, I'm weel enough,' said Tam, stretching the arms which were still brawny. 'But I was wondering, Eppie, my joe, how you would like if we had to go back to the beginning and commence afresh, as we did sax-and-twenty years syne, with a room or twa, and no so muckle as a servant lass; only me to earn our daily bread, and only you to keep the house richt, and spend my wages.'

'Fine, Tam, I would like it—real fine!' exclaimed Eppie, with honest readiness and gladness. 'I dinna pretend that I'm as soople as when I was young, or that I would not miss mony a thing, for ane soon learns ill lessons; but to have you all to mysel' again—to cook for you, to mend for you, and to keep all richt and ticht for you without any help—I could do it as well as ever, and prood to do it, my lad! It would make up for a gude wheen losses.'

And the husband and wife looked into each other's faithful eyes, grasped each other's honest hands, and he knew that she spoke no more than the truth. Each was dear as ever to the other, and so long as the one treasure was left, all else might go, without too bitter lamentation.

Young Eppie had been listening in respectful silence to what she, like her mother, judged too grave talk to be lightly dealt with. But now she spoke up with something like a pout:

'And what is to become of me when you two are going to set up house again by your two selves, wanting nobody else to interfere and upset you? Father, mother, I'm here. You seem to have forgotten my very existence. I must say it is not very kind of you.'

The girl spoke more than half in jest, and yet there was a little soreness in her merry tones. The old ties which had been strong as death were loosening from her; but it smote her that they should drop from her in this fashion—that her father and mother should speak of the future even in the lightest imagination, and leave her out of count. She had not expected it from them.

It was not what *he* would have done—he who was above her in rank, and had been used to grand ladies; he could never draw a picture of his coming life in which she was not in the foreground.

'Never fear, bairn,' said auld Tam tenderly; 'where there are father and mother the bairns can never be forgotten—never—even when they've grown to men and women's estate, are heads of houses of their ain, and have flown far from the parent nest. But I've a question to speer of you, too, young Eppie;' and he drew her nearer to him, and made her look into his face. 'What if all this speak of a grand lad and a title, and a Coort and what not, come to nothing some fine morning, after all? Will you blame your father? Will you never smile in his face again? Will you and he never more be happy together, as you were before?'

'Tam, Tam! ye're tryin' the bairn; she's ower young to answer such questions—though maybe you've a richt to judge for her, since she's under age, if so be you can show a reasonable warrant for your judgment, and she'll submit to your lawful authority when she can; for she's not dour [obstinate] or contermacious [refractory]. She's your ain loving, obedient little lass. But how can you, man? Would you plague her as gin she were a patient Grizel and you were a ragin' tyrant? You've no richt—I will not have it, though I am your wife—it's fair cruelty, Tam.'

In truth, little Eppie had grown white and cold, and was trembling in every limb. At last she said in a low choked voice, looking down and plucking nervously at the bent grass:

'Why are you so thrawn [cross] to him, father? He never harmed you. He has a great liking and respect for you, though you're not like his people. Is it just because he likes me that you are so unkind?'

'Bairn—it will not rest with me,' said Tam, with something like a smothered groan. 'It is supposing Sir Hugie draws back, and will have no more to say to you.'

'He will not draw back,' broke in young Eppie, holding her head high, and with a rush of colour back into her white cheeks. 'He'll never be forsworn, whatever happens. You may make me give him up, but Sir Hugo will never give me up.'

'Not with his will, I daur say,' granted Tam, ' or the loon [fellow], though he were a lord, would not be worth a hoast [cough]. But my gentleman may be overborne, highhearted as he is—I'll not deny it. Bools may row so that he cannot control them. He has his mither and his factor to answer to : a young laird is aften sair hadden down by his factor, and no doubt so is an English squire, though he has a " Sir " before his name, by his agent, who stands for his factor. The young man has his credit with his billies [contemporaries] and the inheritance he has to hand down to the next generation to hamper him. Oh, there are mony things to consider that young folk dinna tak' in at a glance and winna believe can weigh against love itsel'.'

'I dinna believe it!' exclaimed auld Eppie indignantly. 'Dinna heed him, my lamb!' she said rebelliously. 'He's no in earnest, though why he should tak' to sic ill joking in this wild pairt, I canna tell. He's no himsel'. This sail in the cauld has been ower hard upon him, that sits so long in a hot office—that's what it is. Come back to the boat, Tam, like a man; and let's hoist sail and hurry hame, and see the doctor in the bygaun.'

But he paid no attention to his wife. He went on like a man in earnest, and a hale man still, determined to ply his daughter with an imaginary case:

'Sir Hugie is no a reckless callant of a ne'er-do-weel to care only for his ain will and pleasure, and he is not just free to make his choice like a common man. He's like a young prince, bound to think on the interests of others. He may be brocht to see—to fancy he sees that it will be best for you and him to pairt.'

Little Eppie sat motionless with her hands locked together in her lap, while the contention between these two who loved her, and whom she loved so well, passed over her head. The eerie October wind and the sad sea-waves seemed to sigh and sob an accompaniment to the strange incomprehensible argument.

'Then, father,' she said, with a break in her soft voice, and a far-away look of misery in her gentle eyes, 'we *will* part. If you and he agree that we ought, what have I to say? What am I, that I should stand up against him and you? We'll do what is right, and God help us all !'

'Haud your tongue this minute, Eppie!' cried her mother. 'There's no call for you to say such words. Make no rash promises. Oh! it is no fair to bring the bairn here to a place so lonesome that one might commit a murder and it would never be found out till the day of doom, where there's nane but me to interfere between you, and speak her round and break her heart, and get her to give up her lad—a grand lad and a gude lad. You that were so fond o' little Eppie, Tam. You maun have taken leave of your senses—you maun be fey, if ever man was.'

'Never, gudewife,' said auld Tam gruffly, in order to hide a little tremulousness in his own accents. 'You micht trust me, woman, at this time of the day. It's all fair, and will soon be aboon-board. As for you, my bairn, that last word was spoken like my gude little lass, and is a help to her father, as she will like to hear and to think long after he's laid in the mools. It's God's truth as weel. We'll do what's richt an' shame the deevil, and trust to the Pooers aboon, who made baith the city and the solitary places, for the rest. There, think nae mair of what I've been saying. I've been trying you baith, as mother says, and thank God you've neither of you been found wanting, which is nae mair than I looked for, though it's far mair than a sinfu' man deserves. Let's be happy when we can,' cried auld Tam, a little incoherently. 'What would you say, little Eppie, to a race ower the stanes or among the bent? No? Then we'll just take our time—it's all our ain the day—and daunder down to the sma'-boat and row back to the yacht with a gude appetite for the next meal. What will you wager that I've not forgotten in this ploy of idle-set [idleness] whether it's luncheon, dinner, or supper? Never mind; it will be welcome, whatever.'

The women were not so easily set at rest. They were disturbed and dumfoundered; but auld Tam recovered so entirely from the agitation he had shown, he was so much more at his ease from that minute, so resolutely calm and cheerful, that the two Eppies could not help regaining their spirits—though they did not forget—and being as happy once more as the sea and the dread of storms would let them.

The next day was the last day of the trip, and as it was also Sunday, auld Tam, like a reverent Scotchman of the old school, the member of a kirk and a regular attender at the same, caused his vessel to lie-to in a safe anchorage, went ashore in the morning with his party, and walked to the most primitive of parish churches, where he worshipped with his fellow-men. The afternoon was grey, but still calm and quiet. The family group gathered on the deck once more.

Auld Tam made little Eppie read 'a lesson' out of her Testament, as she had done every Sunday when she first began to read, to her father and mother, who had listened with pleased attention and secret admiration that did not prevent their being ready with a homely correction whenever she mispronounced a word. The childish voice had sounded as if it came from a cherub oracle, uttering, without comprehension, in a clear, unfaltering treble, awful words of everlasting moment. The girlish tones were deeper, and had more rising and falling meaning in them; but they were almost as unconscious, with no subtle undercurrent of reflection, as the reader, on this October afternoon, chose for a lesson the history of Jonah, the secret sinner who concealed his superior knowledge, kept back his heaven-sent tidings, and imperilled by his guilty presence an innocent ship's crew.

'He came to his senses, and spoke out like a man at last,' was auld Tam's single comment on the reading, uttered as if the final atonement afforded him great satisfaction.

Then he made young Eppie sing two of the old Scotch psalms. One of them was 'The Lord's my Shepherd,' with its broad distinctions and wide stretches — from death's dark vale, where the Almighty's rod and staff are the sole stay for the forlorn wayfarer, to the sumptuous earthly table furnished in the presence of his human foes, with the kingly oil and the overflowing cup anointing and confirming him as a prince and ruler over his fellows.

Tam, like most Scotchmen of his generation, had said that psalm when a child at his mother's knee.

The other psalm he and his wife had sung together in the congregation on many a peaceful Sunday, but never with such vivid realization as now, when they heard it in the amphitheatre of mountains:

> 'I to the hills will lift mine eyes,
> From whence doth come mine aid.'

As young Eppie sang 'with grave, sweet melody' the solemn, familiar words, the skipper and his men in their Sunday clothes hanging about the deck, and putting a touch now and then to the tackle, which, like a living creature, must be seen to Sunday and Saturday, paused to listen, and took their pipes out of their mouths as if to hear better, though they were too blate [bashful] to draw nearer, or make any other sign of appreciation:

'Behold He that keeps Israel,
He slumbers not nor sleeps.'

No more than these giant sentries, hemming in and protecting the great loch, with nothing hidden there that should not be revealed, and nothing really to fear from a brave revelation.

'Ay, the hills are grand,' said Tam emphatically. 'Grand, like truth itsel'. No mortal lee, or pridefu' conceit, or blind self-deception, will lift up its head before them. I verily believe they're the tabernacle of the Almichty.'

Certainly there was, while he spoke, a light as from a divine sanctuary on Tam Drysdale's face, which had grown so grey and lined of late. The light still lingered upon it when he landed in common day with his womankind at Greenock on the morrow, and was met by the same friends who had escorted him on board, with congratulations on his prosperous trip, to which he responded cordially.

Nevertheless auld Tam continued to

hold off Sir Hugo—not angrily or sternly, rather with a half-authoritative, half-deprecating manner, that seemed to say, 'Not yet, Sir Hugie; wait a little longer, my fine young gentleman, till you see and hear everything.'

CHAPTER XXXVIII.

THE LAST OF RORY OF THE SHELTIES—DR. PETER ON THE SCENT.

'He's gane, and nae mistake, puir lad, said Sandy Macnab, respectful for once, and also for once deficient in his constitutional volubility.

He stood with Dr. Peter Murray by a box-bed far from tidy, but not deficient in the ordinary comforts of a bed of its class, while over the rest of the bedclothes was thrown a tartan plaid. Beneath the covering, with the head and chest exposed, lay the worn, breathless body of Rory of the Shelties, from which life had just departed.

The locality was no remote shieling in

North Uist, but Bawby Sed's house in a street off the Gallowgate of Glasgow. Bawby herself, with the effusiveness of her nature and race, was rocking to and fro, and wailing, with an apron thrown over her head, as if it were her man Andry and her whole numerous family that had been taken from her, instead of a half-witted Highland 'gangrel' (tramp) —who was nobody's body, with whom she had been accidentally and temporarily associated, not greatly to her profit or pleasure.

The time was yet so early in the morning that the November daylight was still only struggling with a tallow candle burning down and guttering in the socket. The fact that the daily life of Glasgow was not far advanced accounted for the comparative privacy and stillness of Bawby's dwelling. The husband and elder children had set forth to their work, and the younger fry had not begun to stir. No visitor was yet ready to drop in, while the old woman who had shared with the mistress of the house the last night-watch by the sick man, had gone out for more assistance to perform with due ceremony, such as Bawby would not on any account have neglected, the office of 'straiking the corp.'

'There's nothing to be done, as you say, Sandy,' remarked Dr. Peter, failing to reproach Sir James Semple's man, who had rushed out to Barley Riggs in the small hours for the doctor, and dragged him in to Glasgow, where medical men abounded, and there was a special practitioner told off for the wants of the poor in the parish in question.

'I thocht, as he had been your patient aince, doctor, you would like to see the last of him,' said Sandy confidentially.

'Well, if it is any comfort to you and the honest woman that I am here, that is something, since I can be of no use to him,' said Dr. Peter resignedly. 'But what was the poor creature doing here, Macnab? I thought he went back to his part of the country, after he was put out of Gartnavel—three—no, I'll be bound it is nearer five months ago.'

'That's just the way of it, sir,' said Sandy, a little confused, but without proceeding to explain how the contradiction came about. Then he turned with some impatience to his lamenting countrywoman. 'I wish you would haud your wheest, Bawby; you will be enough to drive a man doited, with your bubblin' and greetin'!'

'Oh, the puir lad!' went on Bawby, with unabated energy, behind her apron; 'and I thocht when I saw him first that he would bring me word of the auld man —M'Leish, you ken—that befriended me when I was a motherless bairn, and, instead, the lad's ain friends will be wondering what has become of him this day— ochone! ochone!'

'If you would only listen to reason, woman, before you're in the ecsties [hysterics],' remonstrated Sandy; 'what friends is he likely to have, a wasp of a natural—that I should say sic a word and him no cauld—weel on for forty? They will think theirsel's weel quit o' him, I doubtna; forbye, he spoke of no friends save his granny—and she, if she were to the fore, would be weel on to a hunder, ower auld and cauld to care for ocht but the keepin' in o' her ain wee glimmer of life and heat. He cared mair for his bit boxie, when it had the papers intil't, than for a' the friends that ever had the misfortune to own him. As for Ballachulish and auld M'Leish—are you as daft as he was? How could a man from the islands bring you word of what was done on the mainland?'

'Why did he not go back to his island, and where is the box that he set such store on?' inquired Dr. Peter.

He was not a suspicious man, nor was he inclined to believe that a man in Sandy Macnab's position, with a place and a character to lose, would be likely to risk them for what, after all, must have been a small temptation. Still the listener did not quite like the aspect of affairs.

'That's just what it is, sir,' Sandy repeated his vague formula, looking yet more embarrassed. Then the man seemed to take a sudden determination, and resolve on a free confession. 'Losh! I'll tell you a' about it. I havena been so far to blame, nor has Bawby here, that we should beat about the buss [bush], and think shame, and maybe called in question for what we never did or thocht to do. It was not my blame that Mr. Drysdale wouldna give me speech o' him, or he micht have kenned lang syne that the puir sorry Rory was not aff the carpet, but was lying here getting waur and waur, and failing ilka day, till he was as gude as in the death-thraw [death-struggle]. Nicol Macnicol would have naething to say to sic a cargy on board his boat. It would have turned the stamachs of all the fine gentry to see or hear tell of a deeing beggar on the same planks with them.'

'It was to give the craytur a bit treat out of his notie that we keepit him at first,' mourned the more ingenuous Bawby. 'He had never seen Glasgy afore; and then, when he took a turn and fell ill again, and couldna be lifted, I couldna cast him out like a dug, you ken. I'm sure I've had fash [trouble] enough wi' my man Andry —wha's that dour, dornach [strong cloth] is naething to him. He threepit I micht as weel keep beggars' ludgins at aince. And wha's to bury the puir silly chap that's stiffening fast, I canna just say. Sandy Macnab's willing to help. I've some savings in the fit of a stocking that Andry's never seen, or he would have them awa' to put into a society in a jiffy—Andry is an awfu' hand at societies. But I'm willing to waur [spend] a pickle on a Hielantman, and I hope the pariss will do the rest.'

'I'll see to that, Mrs. Seth,' promised Dr. Peter, 'and I'll give you a certificate for the registrar. But you've never told me where the poor fellow got the note on which he was to have had the treat, or where the box is that he valued so highly. Perhaps its contents may be of some consequence to his friends, or may help to defray the expenses of the funeral.'

'Very like!' said Sandy Macnab, not aware of displaying any want of feeling by speaking in a tone of unmistakable derision. 'Yonder the kistie is;' and he pointed to the wayfarer's battered knapsack kicked below a table. 'When it was fu', its valuables consisted, if you'll believe me, sir, of a wheen papers, an auld will of ane Drysdale, and the purpose of marriage of ane Mackinnon, baith of them, I'm creditably informed, dead and buried mair than a score of years syne. I cannot tell what maggot came into Rory's head, but I did the best for him. I got him speech of Mr. Drysdale up at Drysdale Hall, and it was him that, sensible gentleman though he is, gifted Rory with the note in exchange for the papers. I was to see him aff the Broomielaw,' acknowledged Sandy reluctantly, with a slight deepening of his ruddy colour; 'but you see, sir, as Bawby said, it seemed but richt that the craytur should have a treat afore he gaed back to the hills—the mair so that he hadna taken in a particle of what he had seen, but was brodent on some miserable cruivie in North Uist. It seemed an awfu' shame to send him back where he cam' from, with no more notion of the world than that. But for all the gude that it has done to him, and considering what has happened,' said Sandy candidly, as he looked down regretfully on his unfortunate countryman, lying for ever prostrate, 'we micht have left him in ignorance to daunder [saunter] hame in time to dee there.'

Dr. Peter's whole aspect had undergone a change while Sandy spoke. First a startled and then a troubled look came into the thoughtful eyes, until the whole face fell indescribably. At last his mouth set with a rueful determination, and he turned away.

By the time Dr. Peter had ridden out to Barley Riggs he had composed his countenance and rid himself of every trace of disturbance. But it was a very grave, sobered-looking man who presented himself at Athole's breakfast-table, instead of the cheery philosopher who was wont to take his place there, and be the light of the morning and of the meal.

Athole, who had parted from her father overnight in his usual spirits, did not know what to make of the change. She inquired in turn for every patient she could remember, and received no information which could explain Dr. Peter's mood. She investigated into his own health, and was told, with the impatience of a man to whom it was a contemptible trifle at that moment, that he was perfectly well. What should ail him?

'Then I wish, father, people would not call you out during the night when they might do it to as much purpose during the day,' she said discontentedly, looking at the kidney he had hardly touched. 'You may be as strong as Hercules, but facing the darkness and cold at your age does not seem to improve your appetite.'

She expected him to shake himself up and ask jestingly how old she thought him, and whether he was not as good yet for night-work as any young 'swankie' among them. Instead, he muttered gloomily, 'What did it matter? And it had happened to be the morning and not the night — a fine enough morning for the season of the year—but though it had been mirk midnight or in the thick of a snowstorm or a thunderstorm, sickness and sorrow, misery and shame, did not wait for daylight and fine weather.'

Then it struck her that she had never seen him look like that before since she was a child, when she had a dim recollection of the arrival of a letter which had caused her father's face first to flush purple and then to pale to an ashen-grey, and he had drooped his head and not raised it, but gone softly for many a day. She had heard, years afterwards, when the penalty had been paid twice over, and she was old enough to understand, that one of her brothers abroad had got into disgrace, and their father had discharged the debt.

'What is it, father?' Athole now asked plainly, putting her hand in his, and looking wistfully into his face. 'I am old enough now to know, whatever it is. Let me bear it with you!'

He put her gently from him this time. 'It is not what you think, lassie. It is nothing with which we have to do, thank God! Walter is all right now, and so I trust are Sandy, and Mary and Lizzie's husbands. It is no secret of mine, else I dare say I might tell it to you; for, as you say, you are old enough, and you have a woman's wit to help a man in a strait what to do next. But the tale is not mine to tell, as I said before, and you're likely to hear it soon enough,' he ended, with a quick sigh.

Athole was dying to hear at once, but she could not force the confidence which was not his, but some other person's; she could only beg him not to vex himself too much by taking other people's trials upon him. They were not his; he was not called upon to suffer heavily for them, any more than he was answerable for other people's errors.

'Ay,' he said sorrowfully, 'but lookers-on have painful duties to perform sometimes. Do you know, Athie, I have had ere now to go to a friend—one of the oldest and best I had—and tell him something of which he had not the faintest suspicion, that he had a deadly disease upon him and his hours were numbered. If he wanted to settle his worldly affairs and arrange for his family, or to make his peace with his Maker, the present moment was the time, for the obligations of the case admitted of no delay. I have had to go to another friend and give him his choice—a doubtful operation, against which flesh and blood recoiled, or his life lost for a certainty. Yet I would rather undertake either of these commissions twice over, than face what I have to do to-day.'

Her face paled in sympathy with his. Her great grey eyes opened widely; she did not protest further or ply him with remonstrances which would have been so many subtle questions; she stooped and kissed him, but said no more. She watched him go, and went about her ordinary household duties. But all the time she was praying silently for souls in trouble, and that every hair of the heads of all the family at Drysdale Hall might be kept in safety, though the name had never been mentioned in the conversation, and she could not tell what evil one or all of them had compassed, or what harm might befall old or young in the household.

CHAPTER XXXIX.

THE SACRIFICE.

AULD TAM was loitering with his son on the terrace at Drysdale Hall—a favourite place for loiterers and smokers, weather permitting. Though it was November, it was that rare experience in Scotland, a St. Martin's summer. The fields were bare, the trees were leafless, but there was a blue sky overhead and a pale sunshine all around, having a pathos in it, because it was so strange and so fleeting. The shadows were long, and the light fell not upon waving cornfields and rich pasture, full foliage, the flowers of spring and summer, or the fruit of autumn—but upon brown earth, faded grass, the thin blades of winter wheat, and bare boughs more in keeping with the gloom of grey clouds and the biting breath of gales laden with stinging sleet, for which the world was ready. It was like an amnesty between summer and winter, a last herald of peace before the war of the elements, which should rage, with interludes of sullen and hollow truce, from Michaelmas to Candlemas and a 'bittock' beyond.

The Drysdale men had returned together, at the elder's suggestion, rather early in the afternoon, had reported themselves to the women, and were lingering for the sunset as if the month had been May.

Auld Tam's eyes had taken a long range from the bleachfields to the boundaries— not merely of the old farm, but of such 'pendacles' or odd bits of crofts as he had added, field by field, to his property during the last ten years. He had pushed his hat far back on his head, as if the brim might have interfered with his view. He stood now with his big massive forehead exposed in the sinking light illuminating the two faces, as only the setting sun will light them up.

'It's a bonnie pairt,' said Tam Drysdale, with a long-drawn sigh from a full heart; 'a fine bit of country. I'm not sure that mair lines of bleachfields might not be laid out along the whole course of the Aytoun Water, for bleaching and dyeing, even in bad times, are more profitable by a long chalk than farming nowadays. But the land is not ours to do with as we like.'

'Not ours?' echoed young Tam, puzzled; and then, thinking that he had caught his father's meaning, 'Not all ours, of course. We are not nearly monarchs of all we survey. Yonder is Gray of Rintoul's offices, and Sir James's land, while all on the other side is the Duke's. That is the disadvantage of a wide view. If the prospect had been sufficiently circumscribed we might have flattered ourselves that we possessed the earth—so much of it as our eyes rested upon.'

'But as it happens none of it is ours, Tam, my man,' said auld Tam, speaking low and slow, as he reluctantly rose to the task of breaking the truth to his son.

'What do you mean, father?' asked young Tam, in fresh perplexity. 'Times are not so bad as that comes to. I dare say you are uneasy about the Pierrots'—referring to a foreign firm with which Drysdale and Son had considerable dealings that was held in danger in these hazardous times. 'You should know, but I am persuaded they will pull through, and at the worst their assets will cover a large proportion of the loss. Then Mackinlays have come out strong. I cannot fancy your losing heart. Is it not late in the day to do so? Are there not signs—I heard you pointing them out yourself the other morning—that trade is on the turn, or will be before long?'

Young Tam spoke remonstratingly, encouragingly, and all the time with a disturbed wonder that he should have to do so to his father, who stood looking at him fixedly. The sun had gone down now, and there was a shadow on the face which had been lit up a moment before.

'Just so, lad; I have told others that, and I have said the same to myself. It is true in the main, if that were all; but it mak's little odds to them that are powerless to profit by it. Tam, it's not to Pierrots' creditors, or for any other trade obligation, that the land and the works are forfeit. It is to that offisher lad Mackinnon, who has never done a hand's turn, or his father before him, to deserve them.'

Young Tam stared a second longer, then his eyes fell with his heart, and that sank like lead. There flashed upon him with painful clearness and coherency, as in a strong chain of evidence, all the unaccountable changes in his father's behaviour lately—his sudden ageing and listlessness; his fit of restlessness and gaiety, especially unlike the man; his capricious treatment of Sir Hugo Willoughby; his unseasonable yacht trip, in which he would allow no friends except his wife and younger daughter to accompany him. He had appeared to come back from it better, but that very morning Mrs. Drysdale had dropped some words to her son which had suggested that his father had said or done something, in the course of their absence, that had struck her as singular behaviour.

All pointed to one conclusion, the most melancholy and terrible, short of the committal of crime, that can overtake a man.

'You mean,' said young Tam, speaking on the spur of the moment, on a desperate chance, with a sickly smile and a faltering tongue, 'that Mackinnon might have been master here, and that he is still not unwilling to reap some of the fruits of your success. But there are two at a bargain-making, if you decidedly object, which I've sometimes doubted lately. Come, father, we are staying out too long, considering it is November. We shall be having my mother out to look after us presently. She will appear in her cap, or young Eppie will turn up bareheaded. The air is getting chill since the sun went down. I think there will be a touch of frost,' he finished with a slight shiver.

Auld Tam looked into his son's face, which had grown white within the last few minutes, while a nameless apprehension stared out of the scared eyes. Tam Drysdale laughed a dry, harsh laugh, which prompted young Tam instinctively to catch hold of his father's arm. The grip was not shaken off; on the contrary, it was yielded to as part of the play, while auld Tam said plainly:

'You think I'm daft, Tam, and I could find it in my heart to wish I were out of my wits on ae point. For a' that, I'm as wise as I ever was, or am ever likely to be. I can show you paper and penned words; though, puir lad, you'll rue you ever set een on them. In proof of what I've said, c'wa' with me, Tam, to my business-room. There's time enough, or we'll mak' time, for when the thing is to be brocht to licht there need be no further ceremony. It's business, Tam, of the most serious kind, and family hours and rules must be set aside for what will wait for no man. If we're detained after the dinner-hour, we'll send and say we're engaged, and bid the women go on without us.'

Young Tam followed his father full of doubt. He asked himself, and was unable to answer the question, whether this was one of the cunning delusions of madness? He reminded himself, and hated himself for the reminder, as if it were basely dishonourable to auld Tam, who had been master of the situation ever since his son had known him, that contradiction was forbidden in this case, that to humour and soothe the patient was the only possible treatment in the meantime.

But when young Tam was seated at his father's bidding, as if for a prolonged stay in the business-room, and saw auld Tam—without bolting the door to-day—unlock his desk and take out the old papers, the new-comer felt instinctively, with a fresh shock, that there was method in the other's madness, and something tangible in his father's incredible assertion.

It did not take long for young Tam to satisfy himself of the authenticity of Gavin Mackinnon and Margaret Craig's marriage contract and the binding nature of its provision for the heirs. As the young man read for himself, the full consequences of the settlement became instantly present to him, and with it a keen, jarring sense of the irony of fate. In the past he had hastily quarrelled with his lot; he had been displeased to find himself the son of an employer and a rich man. He had said often, and believed the words which he spoke, that he doubted the righteousness of the laws of labour and capital and the distribution of property—that he did not know what to make of the power over his fellow-men which would fall to him. It was as if an evil genius had taken him at his word, deprived him of position and possessions, and freed him from responsibility. But, alas! in the interval which had elapsed he had grown more than reconciled to circumstances. He had taken up and learned to like the calling he was now summoned to abjure. He had begun to build upon it a fine edifice of hope and promise. Young Tam felt small and silly in addition to being ruined with his father. Would Athole Murray, who was so quick to see inconsistencies, have mercy upon him when she knew all? He had been claiming far more than mercy at her hands within these last few happy months—would he sue in his adversity for what she had denied him in his prosperity? He hardly thought so, since he too had his pride, to which he was entitled. It was not pity that he wanted; he felt to-day as if he could not brook pity, however generous, least of all from Athole.

But young Tam had sufficient self-restraint and thought and feeling for others to recognise that this was not the moment for personal regrets, let them be ever so sharp.

'When did you come upon this deed, father?' the young man asked, speaking with unconscious stiffness, which sounded like sternness.

Auld Tam had been standing by the window with his back to his son as he read. Tam Drysdale turned and looked imploringly in the face of his questioner.

'Upon my soul, Tam,' he said solemnly, 'I only came upon the contract by pure accident, two months syne. You will believe me, and I can bring testimony to silence the world if it misdoubt me, which is like enough, on that head. But that does not clear me of wyte [blame]. I ocht to have had common prudence; I should not have been a hot-headed fule; I ocht not to have run the risk of sic a hidden mine being sprung on you and me.'

'It was an oversight,' said young Tam, with generosity in his very bluntness.

'It might have happened to anybody. It cannot be helped.'

'No great time has been lost since the paper was brocht to me—I'll tell you how some other day,' continued auld Tam, still with shamefacedness and deprecation. 'I would have spoken sooner, but I had to battle with the temptation to remain for ever dumb. Oh, laddie, you dinna ken what it has been !' he exclaimed passionately. 'If only truth and honesty could have let me carry the story to the grave, and spare you and the lave [rest] !'

Young Tam got up and wrung his father's hand.

'Never mind us, father; we'll do well enough. We owe you a good education and an honest example.'

'Thanks to you, Tam, for that word,' said his father gratefully.

'I little thocht,' he began again ruefully, 'when I did my best to beguile you into the business, what a burden I was binding on your shouthers. A muckle concern that has broken down and will never be built up again means enough scaith [injury] and scorn to stick to you for life, with your feet catched in a net from which they'll never work themsel's free.'

'Better young shoulders than old to lift the load,' said auld Tam's son loyally; 'and it will be a mess indeed from which I shall not, with you to help me, emerge in time. You do not give me half credit —though you've said as much in words, when it comes to the rub—for having developed some of your business faculty. But this discovery must be seen to immediately,' broke off young Tam, with a sort of brisk severity that had a faint flavour of Dr. Peter in it. 'I suppose Black and Fettes,' naming his father's lawyers, 'had better be spoken to before Mackinnon is told. I don't know much of him. He is not my style of man. I confess I have never seen much in him, either good or bad, and I don't fancy there is much to see; but people seem to think he is a nice enough fellow, so far as he goes. He may take into account how hard this is for you, and how little you were to blame,' said young Tam, with a return of the hope which belongs to youth and comes back with a swiftness of rebound in proportion to the violence of the blow that has laid confidence low. 'Mackinnon may be willing to come to terms —were it only to grant us time. Besides——' young Tam paused. He had the reluctance to speak on the subject which a young man will show to an elder, which the best brothers display when it is their sisters' affairs that are about to be discussed. 'You must have seen for some time, father,' he went on awkwardly, 'that Mackinnon is sweet on Clary.'

'Or on what he tak's to be her siller,' said auld Tam sarcastically.

'I believe that he is attached to her, and that she returns the attachment,' asserted young Tam.

'And you would have us seek to ride out

of our difficulties on the attachment, as you call it, of twa young fules!' said auld Tam, in a mortified voice. 'Weel, I did think to make it up to the young felly in that way; but then he was not to ken—nobody was to ken. I never thocht to be indebted for grace to my dochters' lauds [lovers].'

'No, you would have had it all the other way,' remarked young Tam, unable to restrain a smile in spite of the gravity of the situation. 'I would not have you take advantage of anybody—I'm sure you know that—and I would have it all plain and above-board. Lay everything before him; but do not refuse to let him be just, or even generous. One can stand a man's generosity, if it is in the beggar. Do as you would be done by.'

'I daur say you're richt, Tam,' granted auld Tam, not without a lurking profound admiration for his son's moderation and good judgment, as well as for his rectitude. 'Indeed I have no manner of doubt you are. You see what it is to bring a young head to reason out a thing. There are cases where the young are mair reasonable and liberal than the auld. But it is queer,' he added, musing, ' to be behadden to Gavin Mackinnon's son—to gang cap in hand and beg his forbearance.'

'That is not the way to put it,' objected young Tam ; but he missed the opportunity of putting it in any other way, for at that moment a servant knocked and handed in Eneas Mackinnon's card.

Father and son looked at each other with honest eyes, that yet had a cloud of confusion in them as of two conspirators caught in the act.

Had he found it all out? Who had told him? Had Sandy Macnab betrayed the little he knew? Were the Drysdales to be deprived of the grace of coming forward and producing the deed in his favour, of which nobody except themselves knew, which had been for some time in their hands, so that the possessors might have destroyed it any day, but which they were now prepared to bring to light?

Auld Tam was the first to recover from this additional misfortune, and to anticipate and demolish any plan his son might have made for parleying—admitting nothing and denying nothing till Black and Fettes' advice was given.

'Let him come on,' said Tam Drysdale sturdily, with something of his old hardy independence and dash of pugnacity, now that he had made a clean breast of it to his son. 'If I have done him wrang, I have done you and myself a hantle mair, and we're willing to mak' reparation to our last shilling.'

But the moment Eneas entered it was clear that his intentions were of the most pacific description—that he was the more agitated of the two sides, and in a sense the more humbled—that he had come to ask and not to grant grace.

In truth, the Lieutenant had at last screwed up his courage to put an end to the state of wretched suspense and perplexity in which he had been living—to propose for Claribel Drysdale to her father, knowing all the time with the most excruciating matter-of-factness of conviction, how little the proposal was worth in a mercenary light.

It was a proof of the pitch to which Eneas's nerves were strung that the circumstance of auld Tam's not being alone, but in the company of his son, in place of affording the suitor a welcome if somewhat cowardly excuse to defer the cruel ordeal of the suit to another day, only spurred him on to take the leap from which there was no returning. The desperateness of the position lent the 'heavy swell' calmness, so that it was with a certain dignity approaching to haughtiness that Eneas began, after an ordinary preamble on the weather:

'If you will allow me a few words, Mr. Drysdale—I shall not detain you long. I have admired Miss Drysdale ever since I knew her, though I was aware——'

Here he was summarily interrupted. Many a time had Eneas Mackinnon pictured to himself, with all the anguish of a shy, proud man, the details of that interview. How the rich, self-made man whom Eneas coveted for his father-in-law, to whose homespunness the wooer was fully alive, whom he could not acquit of unvarnished purse-pride, would, in spite of the recent alteration in his behaviour, and notwithstanding all Claribel had said in her father's defence, meet the advances of the penniless lover with unbearable scorn and contumely.

But Eneas had never gone so far as to imagine that he would be peremptorily stopped in his little speech with 'Not another word, sir! I will not hear another word!' or that young Tam, who knew the world, was college-bred, and like other people, except that he had the reputation of being a Radical, should instantly back his father with an imperative 'Yes, Mackinnon, for your own sake, for all our sakes, be silent till you know what you are about.'

Eneas Mackinnon got up from the chair which had been offered to him.

'If you will not so much as hear what I have to say, there is indeed nothing to be done,' he said, roused to indignation by the incredible treatment he was receiving. 'But you will pardon me if I tell you that I think a little courtesy is due to a gentleman and an officer in her Majesty's service, who has done nothing to disgrace his birth and position, though he is a poor man. I owe it also both to myself and to Miss Drysdale, who I am certain would not thank me for any reserve on this point, to let you know that it is not without warrant from her——'

'Haud your tongue, you deevil, when you're telled,' cried auld Tam still more vehemently and unceremoniously, 'or it will be the waur for you! Can you not tak' a hint? Will you not let us leave you the freedom of choice till you hear all?'

Eneas was confounded and disgusted. He was fain to hide his discomfiture and escape from further outrage. He could only make a slight bow, which was a tacit relinquishment of all future intercourse with Claribel Drysdale's father and brother —dear as she was to him—and move to the door. But Tam Drysdale was again before him.

'Ne'er a fit shall you steer till you listen to my story, since you've come in at the nick of time with yours. I'll tak' Black and Fettes into my ain hands, Tam, or see them hanged ! but Lieutenant Mackinnon shall ken what he's about, before he's an hour aulder. He'll not come here any longer courtin' an' speerin' Clary, without first hearing what her father has cost him— unawares, sir—unawares. Let him see the contract, Tam, and then we'll hear whether he sings to a different tune.'

'Don't misjudge us, Mackinnon,' said young Tam apologetically. 'My father has been very much put about lately, and,

I can tell you, so may everybody be when all is known. But if you will look at this paper you will see that it is in your interest, and to prevent your prejudicing it, in ignorance of what you are doing, that we are acting in this manner.'

'Do you ken the deed, Mr. Mackinnon?' asked auld Tam a little more composedly, but yet worked up into a state of excitement which kept him from being silent.

'No,' said Eneas, a little sulkily, still feeling himself an insulted individual, a victim of a poor gentleman, yet not without a dim comprehension that the Drysdales meant better by him in their strange behaviour than he could understand, or perhaps was entitled to expect.

'It is your faither and mither's marriage contract,' said auld Tam, coming to the point at once. 'Did you ever hear tell o't?'

'Yes,' said Eneas, in increased surprise; 'I have heard my aunts in St. Mungo's Square speak of it many a time. We did not know what had become of it; but I never thought it was of any consequence.'

'You were wrang, then,' was Tam Drysdale's short rejoinder; 'but read it for yoursel' noo, when you've the chance, and see what you have to do with it.'

Thus urged, Eneas Mackinnon stood still and read the paper put into his hands, while the two Tams watched keenly his handsome, usually impassive face. It had been working with various emotions before he began to read, and as he read on it was hard to say what of rage or triumph or compunction passed over this page of quivering flesh and blood, while the truth dawned upon Eneas, as it had dawned upon others in turn, that he had been during the whole course of his life unwittingly defrauded of his due—by his own father and mother in the first place, and by Claribel's father in the second.

With the knowledge came also the realization to the Lieutenant—a realization not the less certain that it was a dull, vague pain as yet—of how much he had suffered, what galling poverty for a man in his station he had endured, how cheerless had been his prospects, and how their hopelessness had early broken his spirit and crushed the life in him. And he was standing in the presence of the man who had 'unawares,' as he asserted, flourished on the unfair acquisition of Eneas's birthright, whose son and daughters had succeeded to every advantage inherited by a rich man's children.

Moreover, this rich man—this old servant of Gavin Mackinnon's—had until lately treated Eneas with hardly veiled contempt, so that he had come into Tam Drysdale's company, half an hour before, in almost abject dread of his withering scorn.

The paper rustled in the young man's grasp, and he bent his head over it, till young Tam began to ask himself, and to telegraph with his eyes to his father—was it quite fair after all thus to take their natural enemy by surprise, though he had stepped in upon them unexpectedly, and to subject him, while he was unprepared with the means of baffling their observation, to so searching a scrutiny?

Suddenly Eneas Mackinnon looked up and put down the paper.

'Well?' he questioned coldly, as if he were the very incarnation of caution.

'Weel,' echoed Tam impatiently, in answer to the enigmatical remark, 'are you satisfied that your mither's property is yours—less the purchase-money—in spite of all that is come and gone?'

'It might have been mine, you mean, Mr. Drysdale,' corrected Eneas calmly. 'It was sold and bought before I was born.'

'But dinna you see that the bargain, for which there was no title, is null and void?' demanded Tam almost querulously.

'In law, perhaps, yes; in honour, no. My father had the purchase-money; you bought the place in good faith and made the most of it, which we should never have done. There is an end of the matter.'

'Well, you're a gentleman and no mistake,' said auld Tam, with sudden conviction.

'I hope so,' said the Lieutenant, with his ordinary quietness; 'not that I have given any great example of it here'—he hastened to guard against exaggeration and bathos, which are the peculiar horror of men of his stamp. 'I might, indeed, resent losing a chance in trade which has been a splendid one in your hands; but it was lost mainly, on the face of the transaction, by my father and mother's blindness, and I have not been so wise on my own account as to take it upon me to condemn the blunders of my progenitors. Besides, I could not have made a kirk or a mill of the works which have prospered so well with you. As it happens I'm in the army, for better, for worse; and if I'm little good as a soldier, I should do still less in any other character. What would you have?' He finished as if he would say, with a curious proud sincerity, 'Where is there any particular merit in what I'm doing? and I'm not going to take credit for what I don't deserve.'

But both auld Tam and young Tam contradicted him.

'I'm proud to know you, Mr. Mackinnon, sir,' insisted Tam Drysdale, in perfect earnestness and simplicity. 'Ay, though I'm free to own I've bocht the knowledge at a heavy cost. You're come of a gude auld stock, and you do it honour. Eh! Clary was aye a wise lass—I micht have kenned that.'

At these words the Lieutenant softened.

'I am glad you think so, sir,' he said, and he even gave a little nervous laugh. 'Will you tell her so? Will you prove your faith by your deeds?'

'That will I,' answered auld Tam fervently.

But young Tam was waiting to speak.

'I trust, Mackinnon, you give us credit for being, to the best of our ability, honest men. As such it is impossible for us to let the business rest here. It must be put into the lawyers' hands. If a compromise can be effected, well and good; we shall be only too thankful, for I need hardly point out to you that, to men in business, anything else would be about the greatest misfortune that could befall them. If— after matters are settled,' young Tam stammered, for he too had to struggle with mingled pride and better feelings, 'you should still wish to be connected with us, I for one will be very glad.'

'I thought matters were settled,' said Eneas half loftily, half languidly, 'when Mr. Drysdale was good enough to praise your sister for wisdom in the most foolish thing she has ever done. But if my future relations will think the best of me,' he added in an easier, more friendly tone—' I hope they will not be disappointed—and if they will offer me a welcome, I need not say I am greatly obliged to them.'

'Say no more,' interposed auld Tam.

'Clary has known best—we have great cause to endorse her opinion and thank her for it. I'll tell her so with my ain lips; and although she has a mind of her ain, as a lassie so by ordinar' sensible has a richt to have, she'll be pleased to hear her father say so. Her mother will neither be to haud nor bind; and little Eppie, who has been looking at me with beseeching een for weeks past, will be as prood as gin you were Sir Hugie, whose turn will come next. There's the denner-bell; you'll dine with us, sir—of course you will. Dress? What's dress among friends? The very Queen on the throne looks ower't on occasions. Forbye, you offishers' worst coats have an air that is wanting in we ceety men's best.'

CHAPTER XL.

A NICE CALCULATION.

DR. PETER had *carte blanche* to dine at Drysdale Hall on every day of the year. If his plate was not always laid for him, it was ready to be brought when he wanted it. He might even come in at any stage of the dinner, and in spite of his protestations have the soup and fish recalled for his special benefit, while the rest of the company waited cheerfully, and the success of the other courses was risked without a groan, so heartily was he welcomed. But he had certainly never contemplated breaking bread with Tam Drysdale this day.

The truth is, there are more things than

business which will not tarry till a man has his way. Among these matters are the physical ills that flesh is heir to. The popular poor man's doctor, in a crowded district, is pretty sure to be intercepted and turned aside from his goal, at the very time that he is most anxious to avoid interruption and keep faith with himself. Dr. Peter durst not defer his errand to another day, and so he brought it to the dinner-table at Drysdale Hall, where he found the little pleasant stir and excitement which betokens a happy family event on the eve of its fulfilment. The very servants were sensible that something of the kind was going on. Though Mr. Mackinnon had dined frequently of late with the Drysdales, the subordinates had an impression that this off-hand dinner was not like the other dinners, but was a prelude to enlarged family gatherings without end.

There were bright faces round the table, among which Claribel's showed a calm superiority to girlish tremors, while the Lieutenant's was equally free from all save an air of relief, and a mild basking in the rays of his sun.

Young Tam's looked the most pre-occupied face, with an occasional knit of the brows as if he had mental nuts to crack.

The atmosphere round auld Tam was that of rest for the time, not of warfare over; for he knew the battle was to re-commence to-morrow, a tough enough contest still, to render it doubtful to which side victory might incline. But when had auld Tam shrunk from a tussle with fortune, or when had he feared to be beaten unless where he was hedged about with such fatal casualties and inopportune disasters that no man could have overcome them? But the hedge was broken down, and the rough way made clear again, and what man could do he would, with his son Tam fighting by his side. Only to-day, Tam Drysdale had a breathing-space to recover from the weariness which had threatened to be deadly. It was rapidly passing away before the first breath of open air, light, and liberty, when a man speaks out what ought to have been proclaimed on the housetop, but has lain hidden in secret places; when he consents to pay his penalty like a man, and reviving heart and hope answer instantly to the proper treatment of the disease, as the steel to the magnet, as the green earth to the sun and rain.

Dr. Peter did not know what to make of the scene. How could auld Tam sit like a patriarch crowned with honour and well-doing, considering what was on his conscience? How had he the face, the heart to entertain his victim? Nay, it was plain that Tam Drysdale intended to perpetrate a further piece of iniquity by allowing Eneas Mackinnon to marry Claribel, by making him one of the family, a sharer in their prosperity and adversity, in order to shut his mouth if there was ever any suspicion of the truth.

Did young Tam know anything of the unpardonable tampering with law and justice? Could he have been suborned and seduced into crooked paths? He was more silent and glummer than in his hobbledehoy days. He looked harassed, almost careworn. Here was another stab to Dr. Peter, for he had been fond of that lad, fonder than he knew. Young Tam too! Dr. Peter's righteous soul sickened with repugnance and shame. Auld Tam noticed that his friend was not himself, and, as Athole had done in the morning, pressed him with sympathetic inquiries after patients who were in a better case than their doctor was.

If Dr. Peter had but retained sufficient faith in auld Tam and in his Maker, a good many hours of wretchedness and useless mortification would have been saved. Peter Murray might have known that Tam Drysdale's long life of reverence and integrity would not go for nothing, that it is not such as he who make shipwreck of conscience and character, and trample religion and morals under foot, midway in their career. He might have guessed that if auld Tam slipped and fell, it would only be to rise again and mount to greater heights, though it were through the valley of humiliation.

If Dr. Peter had but known it, when he was seen to pass the dining-room window, auld Tam's eyes had sparkled with eager satisfaction. He had murmured to his son:

'It's like a play, Tam, ilka player dropping in at the precise moment to fit into the performance, to hear what concerns him, and act his part in the drammy.'

He was in reality burning for the ladies to be gone, to leave him and the two young men and Dr. Peter, who had his interest in the business—with regard to which he was about to be enlightened—to go into it afresh. The opening it up to young Tam had been like the letting out of waters, and auld Tam, having liberated the flood, was not disposed to try the vain experiment of damming it up again. For that matter, he laboured under a fit of reaction, with its tendency to rush from one extreme to another, to shout in the market-place what he had hitherto refrained from whispering in the ear.

At Tam Drysdale's first word a load was lifted from Dr. Peter's mind—the horrible load of being compelled to call a friend to account for a miserable departure from duty —and if he would not turn from the error of his ways to denounce him to the world. It was as if he had awakened in an instant from a bad dream, when a whole phantasmagoria of evil motives and unrighteous deeds vanished in the twinkling of an eye. Dr. Peter was ready to thank God and take courage; nay more, to feel affronted because he had done his friend a wrong which it would be impossible to repair by immediately owning it. To tell auld Tam what Dr. Peter had thought of him for the better part of a day would be to add insult to injury. In all their future intercourse there would always be a confidence, shyly withheld on the one side, though auld Tam admitted frankly on the other:

'I was sorely tempet, Peter, if you will believe me, to hide all knowledge of Gavin Mackinnon's contract. You could never credit how I was tempet, God help me! I dinna ken at this moment how the balance might have turned, if it had not been that the twa Eppies were as true as steel, and that I felt that I could not look my laddie Tam in the face again if I gaed for the rest of my life with a lee in my richt hand.'

It was Dr. Peter's punishment for his want of faith that he had to remain silent, hanging his fine head somewhat at this appeal. He would never mention on what errand he had come so opportunely to Drysdale Hall that evening.

Later on Dr. Peter cut his knot of the thread in the tangled web without difficulty:

'You can demand back from me my father's share in the purchase-money you paid for the works. Good. Then I can come upon your future son-in-law—is it not so, Tam?—for his father's having misled mine as to the legality of the sale. In addition, I can try to prove that you owe me a share of your profits during these intervening years, in proportion to my father's share in the concern, and to the state of the works and business when you got them; and you can retaliate by showing that you found the plant falling to pieces, and the dyeing trade at Drysdale Haugh on its last legs—a ticklish contention, which might be very profitable to the lawyers engaged in it, but for the rest of the people who had to do with the suit, I take it the thing would be about square to begin with.'

Sir Hugo Willoughby and Guy Horsburgh looked in during the evening—to complete the *dramatis personæ*, auld Tam kept telling himself, though only Sir Hugo had an interest, and that an indirect one, in the question which was so momentous to the master of Drysdale Hall. The young gentleman had paid his court to little Eppie, believing her to be a rich man's daughter. Sir Hugo's lady-mother —and doubtless the rest of his great relations would follow her example—had consented to put up with the origin of Eppie and her fortune; but what if the fortune disappeared, and the bonnie lass had only her face to depend upon for their favour? What if her father, in place of being honoured in the city, had been covered with disgrace—a man who had held land and works without a warrant, and had so recklessly traded with them that he had ended in becoming bankrupt, to the ruin of many better men than himself? Sir Hugo had still a risk to run, but he might take his chance. He would no longer be able to say that he had been beguiled into an alliance with Eppie Drysdale and with trade under false pretences.

Auld Tam felt so convinced that everything was leading up to a *dénouement*, he took an opportunity to speak a few words aside to his last visitor.

'I'll give you your answer to-morrow, Sir Hugie, if that will please you. I grant you've been patient, and I thank you for it, to what must have seemed to you rank tyranny and a speerit of contradiction. But you'll ken better before you're mony hours aulder. I'll lay my reasons before you, and you'll admit I had cause for what I did.'

'I have no doubt, sir, you acted for the best,' said Sir Hugo, with the most anxious deference, trembling lest he should spoil the propitious moment by any false step. 'I am sure your reasons are excellent, if only you will entertain——'

'Your proposal, and give you my younger dochter,' auld Tam finished the sentence. 'Some things are worth waiting for, and the desire of your heart and a gude wife are among them. Can you blame me that I'm loth to lose her? You've some notion of what kind of dochter she's been, and let me tell you, Sir Hugie, that's the best assurance of the wife she'll mak' to him that gets her—I do not say to you, for there's mony a slip 'tween the cup and the lip. If she's sweet to you, what do you think she maun be to me, who dandled her in my arms—the bonniest and best of weans [babies] from her cradle. How do you think Drysdale Hall will look to me and mother when there's ne'er a young lass to set it out and keep it cheery? You young fellies that come seeking your own ends think little of the blank you leave behind you when you carry the day.'

'Forgive me, sir, I do think of it,' protested Sir Hugo. 'I know that I am selfish, and that I ask far more than I deserve; but if there is anything I can do——'

'Mak' her happy, man,' said auld Tam, 'if she's ever yours, for there are some craws to be pu'd yet between you and me. Mind that it was your will to raise her to your state—if so be she is raised. I've no fear but that she'll make a gentle leddy, for she's that already. Then if you're gude to her, as a man should be to the mate he has chosen out of all the world, her mother and me will bless and not ban you.'

There was a little music and a great deal of talk in the warmth and brightness—for auld Tam went clean against the modern vagary of fashion which prefers semi-darkness to light—and in the flowery fragrance of the Drysdale Hall drawing-room.

Mrs. Drysdale would have willingly foregone her nightly game of bézique, but Eppie would not suffer the omission. Perhaps she had a premonition that her mother would soon have to relinquish that and many another kindly custom dear from old use and wont, doubly dear from mother love. The sole change young Eppie would consent to make was that Sir Hugo might join the game; and in order not to render the privilege too peculiar, she invited his friend Guy Horsburgh to be the fourth in the quartette—a piece of good breeding on account of which Sir

Hugo, with all his virtues, was not above being piqued for the twentieth part of a minute.

Clary was at the piano playing occasionally, with Eneas Mackinnon to turn over her music and talk to her in the intervals.

Auld Tam and Dr. Peter sat on a couch, saying little, simply enjoying the smiling peace of the scene. Tam Drysdale leant back, and had his arms crossed above his head in an easy unconventional attitude, while he stared fitfully into the fire. No contrast could be greater than the air the room presented to the agitated conversation between the father and the son on the terrace in the afternoon, or the breathless explanation with Eneas Mackinnon in the business-room afterwards.

After the storm comes the calm, but one never knows when a bomb-shell may not fall and burst amidst the most tranquil surroundings.

The author of the disturbance on this

occasion was young Tam, who had been sitting buried in an easy-chair, busy with a paper and pencil, as if he were torturing himself and his neighbours by working out a succession of double acrostics. Suddenly he rose with a flushed face and generally excited mien. He walked across to his father, holding up the sum of his calculations.

'Father,' he said, 'when your father's cousin Drysdale, of Drysdale Haugh, died in Scotland, and his niece by marriage and adoption, Mrs. Craig, died at Calcutta——'

Tam put the speaker away with a half-peremptory, half-reproachful gesture.

'Hooly [stop]! Tam, we've had enough of this for one day. Mind, the upshot of the story is not so new to some of us as to you. It must be gone into again presently, and every blessed thing sifted to the bottom. There's no help for that. But I think it is neither judicious nor altogether ceevil to Lieutenant Mackinnon yonder, who has behaved like a perfect gentleman,

A NICE CALCULATION.

for you, while in his company—though he's no heeding—to keep hammering on at the unfortunate transaction in which his father and mother were the maist to blame, and to rake up the slender nature of the connection between his grandmother and auld Drysdale.'

'But I must speak, and the sooner the better,' cried young Tam, not even troubling in his excitement to modulate his voice. 'If the matter be gone into, as it certainly will if I have a voice in it, it cannot be done on mistaken premises. There is something else wrong which must be seen to instantly. You know the period of time that intervened between the deaths of the uncle and niece.'

'It was some twa hours,' said auld Tam, slowly and in a stupefied way, for the events of the day were proving too much for him, while Dr. Peter sat bolt upright and looked all alive. Then auld Tam shook himself up and spoke more definitely; 'auld Drysdale died here—that is, at Drysdale

Haugh — when the knock was chappin' twal', on the 11th of June, as I've heard tell. Mrs. Craig died on the same day, at Calcutta, at twa in the afternoon— twa hours later; and I've been assured that twa minutes langer breath for her would have been enough to constitute her infant her heir.'

'Ay, but I am prepared to show that the advantage is all on the other side. The question is not one of law, but of science, and nobody has seen it in that light. Allowance has not been made for the difference of time in different longitudes. As you count hours by the earth's course round the sun, Mrs. Craig died about an hour and a half before instead of two hours after her uncle.'

'Gude preserve us!' exclaimed Tam, while Dr. Peter started to his feet with an ear-piercing 'Whew!' that caused Eneas Mackinnon at the piano to raise his eyebrows, Clary beside him to shrug her shoulders, and the whole bézique party to pause and look round for an instant.

'You dinna mean it,' said auld Tam almost piteously. 'Is it so?' He turned helplessly to Dr. Peter. 'Are the tables turned? Was I so lang kept out of my ain? Have I been twice wranged and never the wrangdoer?'

'I make little doubt of it. I believe young Tam is right, but I must go over the calculation for myself—it is easy enough—if you will give me a minute. To think the difference of hemispheres never occurred to the lawyers who administered the will! You see what it is to have a son a student—the first in his class in mathematics. Chemistry is not everything, eh, Tam?'

'I wish he had spoken suner,' said auld Tam, with a groan over the anguish from which he might have been spared.

'The calculation never occurred to me any more than to the lawyers who sat upon the will,' said young Tam modestly.

'The astronomical reckoning is, as Dr. Peter says, plain and simple enough. Every schoolboy is taught to make it, though he may not be able to put the knowledge into practice at a moment's notice. I did not think of the old will, which I never saw till to-day.'

'Ca' him here,' said Tam, indicating the 'offisher lad.' 'I'll do to him as I would be done by.'

But Eneas Mackinnon did not receive the last news as he had received the first. He reddened violently at the idea of his mother's having entered upon and disposed of an inheritance which was never hers. He recoiled from the prospect of being made out auld Tam's debtor to an overwhelmingly hopeless extent, instead of Tam's being proved his—Eneas's—debtor to an amount which the young man's generosity and his love for Claribel rendered easily redeemable. His pride and his good feeling had been alike flattered by the power, rare with him, of granting an amnesty and dispensing favours. His slow-working intellect could not readily grasp the astronomical calculation, easy as it was, which was said to overturn the will. Fortune, if not the Drysdales, appeared to be playing strange tricks upon him. It was a return to the old story, and something worse. He was reduced, in the course of a few hours, to his former detested condition of genteel poverty and absence of any chance of independence and moderate prosperity. Added to it, he was already loaded with huge money obligations to auld Tam Drysdale, which Eneas could no more think of retrieving, in the natural term of his life, than he could look forward to receiving the baton of a field-marshal. Auld Tam was wise in his generation. He might not essay what was equivalent to the vain task of taking breeches from a breechless Highlander. He might cancel Eneas's mountain-load of obligations, but neither the obligations nor the cancelling formed a fitting preparation for the poor Lieutenant's figuring as the accepted suitor and future husband of his wise, beautiful Claribel. Was ever reverse more complete, or fresh humiliation more galling? In some lights a greater man is required to be generous in adversity than in prosperity, in order to accept a burden of favour neither greedily nor grudgingly, but graciously. It was not wonderful that Eneas Mackinnon, when his muddled brain became sufficiently clear, spoke stiffly, and even angrily:

'Gentlemen, I do not pretend to be equal to these nice calculations. I am not, to my loss no doubt, a business man. I must really refer you to my lawyer.'

It was to no purpose that auld Tam protested, almost with tears in his eyes:

'It makes no manner of difference, Lieutenant Mackinnon, sir. Do you think I can ever forget how well you behaved to me this very day when you had the ball at your fut? Do you suppose I blame your father and mother any more than you blamed me for what was done in ignorance? Do you believe I hold you accountable for a purchase on my pairt, of which you yoursel' said, since the sun went doon, that it was made in gude faith, and you would stand by it. Sir, your father disposed of Drysdale Haugh as I bocht it, in gude faith; and do you imagine that I would hold his son responsible for the fact that Gauvin Mackinnon, in the name of his wife, sold and I bocht what was my ain all the time, without anybody guessing the truth? I was pleased to get the place on his terms, I never grudged them—I have made my own of them, and will do it again when trade turns. I'll hold myself bound to charge the land and the works with my eldest dochter's tocher, and I'll give it and her to you as a free gift with all my heart, because I'm proud to waur her and her bawbees on a real gentleman such as I said you were this afternoon, and I'll say it again with my last breath.'

In vain Dr. Peter chimed in with the

dim recollection of another extraordinary factor in this medley of law and justice.

'I've a notion,' he said, 'that if property is held for the space of forty years or thereabouts, by other than the rightful owners, through some mischance—like this of mistaken time—then a law called 'the law of proscription' steps in and bestows the property on the holder, forbidding a restoration to rightful heirs that leaps over more than one generation. It is upwards of forty years since Mrs. Craig's child's title to Drysdale Haugh was made out, and that title has never been challenged, to the best of my knowledge, till now. On the other hand, Mrs. Mackinnon did not keep the place in her possession for much more than half the specified time. She sold it to the lawful heir. I cannot tell what to make of it, Tam; it beats me.'

It was Clary who settled the question when she came over and asked what they were all talking over so earnestly, and was told as well as so complicated a story could be conveyed in a few words. She thought a little, and then gave her decision without hesitation :

'Let well alone, let matters be as they are : my father could not, if he wished it, exact from Mr. Mackinnon a forfeit which no officer without a large private fortune could pretend to pay. And what could Mr. Mackinnon make of the Drysdale Haugh works, if the law were to decree them to him, while the farm without the dyeing and calico-printing would not, in the present state of agriculture, support the old farmhouse, if it could be restored, stripped of the modern mansion. Let everything remain as it is. I take it for granted,' she ended, looking up with a little smile at Eneas, ' the law will not put us all in prison, as it did your aunts in St. Mungo's Square, because we decline to avail ourselves of its costs and surprises and delays.'

While successions were thus bandied, fortunes turned upside down, and lives reversed, the bézique-players, in utter unconsciousness of what was going on in the same room, proceeded with their play—shuffling and dealing their cards, pairing their couples, running up their rows of figures. It was as if the four were typical players, engaged in the same game of life which was being enacted in another form, without their knowledge, by their side, and that the counters in reality were human heads and hearts.

CHAPTER XLI.

ATHOLE MURRAY SKETCHES A MODERN FUG-
GEREI—THE MISS MACKINNONS' ULTIMATUM.

ATHOLE MURRAY did not see her father for the next twenty-four hours. He lingered at Drysdale Hall till it was late, not returning to Barley Riggs till she had reluctantly retired—ostensibly to rest, actually to pass a sleepless night. She would fain have sat up for him, but did not like to disobey his orders on this night of all others. He had to start by break of day to attend a professional consultation which was to be held at some distance. He was detained longer than he expected, took the round of his patients on his way home, and did not reappear at Barley

Riggs till Athole's tea-hour, when he walked in almost simultaneously with auld and young Tam.

In the interval Athole had got sufficient time to brood over what she had made out of his conversation the previous day, with the conclusion she had leaped to of calamity, not unmingled with disgrace, hanging over the Drysdales. She could not fathom it, but the impression was there. When the blow fell, would her relations be the same to young Tam? All her heart was melting to him to atone for the injustice of fortune and the injury inflicted by another, though she knew not by whom. She had been fond of auld Tam. She could not lightly think evil of him, though she had been sorely perplexed by his conduct lately; but at least young Tam was blameless, honourable, and trustworthy—she could swear to that. She felt all at once impelled to comfort him, with a soft but irresistible impulse which no force could stay.

While she was in this mood the three

men walked in upon her, full of their strange story of a marriage contract, and a last will, of lost documents, and overlooked problems of science, restitution, and compromise. The speakers were all eager, and, as it seemed to her in her shaken spirits, all rejoicing to the verge of exultation. They were so bent on telling her their story, and so sure of her sympathy, that they did not miss it when it failed to flow forth as it ought to have done; nobody said, as he might have said, 'You are not answering—you are not glad; what has come over you?'

Young Tam would have been the last to do it, for he was the most carried away, the gayest. He seemed taken out of himself, as he stood there like a victor in the flush of victory, to whom all must yield.

And do what Athole would, she who was still thrilling with the sense of what she had almost made up her mind to be to him if he were the loser, who was dragged two ways between a sense of blank disappointment at the instantaneous fading away of the vision which in a night had grown so sweet and a feeling of intense pride and pleasure for his sake, that his hand had cut the knot and rescued auld Tam from his strait, could not for her life resist young Tam's new attitude as a conqueror. Her eyes fell before his. Her colour went and came; she could not laugh, she could not speak, she did not know how long she would be able to breathe. Her hands trembled so that she had to clasp them tightly to keep them still. She felt the ground slipping from beneath her feet.

Her father was the first to remark upon her silence.

'Is there anything the matter with you, Athie?' inquired Dr. Peter, like a grey-headed *enfant terrible,* and then he wound up with the *mal à propos* remark, 'You are not like yourself.'

Auld Tam tapped his friend on the arm:

'Come awa', man; we are twa ower mony. Leave her to a younger doctor.

Dod! did you never suspect that the wind blew in that quarter?' in answer to the look of bewilderment, enlightenment, tender regret, and unselfish satisfaction with which his hint was met. 'There is nane so blind as a clever, honourable gentleman.'

When the pair were beyond hearing, auld Tam had his joke out of the situation.

'You'll never have the face to object now, Peter, when you've given the lad every encouragement—treated him as if he had been a son of your ain, from the time he went after your lassie.'

'I cannot leave my father, and I'll never be able to look your mother in the face. You know she cannot abide me,' protested Athole to young Tam.

'You will not be far from your father,' he told her; 'and as for my mother, when she sees that you give me more than my due, and finds what you can do for her son, she will not know how highly to prize you. Besides, you are going to make up to her for the loss of Clary and Eppie.'

'Are you so mad as to think I shall ever be like little Eppie—like Lady Willoughby of Willoughby Court—to your mother?'

'You will fill your own place as young Mrs. Tam, to whom my mother will pay all respect. I say, Athole, you can afford to be second best with her. You are the style of woman who can consent to that.'

If Athole was likely to be second best with mother Eppie, there was every indication of her holding her own with auld Tam, when before he left she sketched for him a Glasgow version of the Augsburg Fuggerei, a Drysdale quarter of St. Mungo's city, built expressly for the accommodation of the working classes, which he vowed if he rose above trade troubles he would rear as a memorial of his deliverance from a great temptation and a great downfall.

'And young Tam's initials shall be intertwined with yours, Athole, and wrocht beneath mine and Eppie's aboon ilka door.'

The Lieutenant hesitated whether the two discoveries in relation to the marriage contract and the will should be communicated to his aunts. He was not at all sure how they would take the news. But Claribel advocated entire openness.

'They are entitled to hear,' she said. 'Besides, they will only believe what they like; and they will remain convinced that they did the best for you and everybody. So far as intentions went, I am sure they are right.'

Claribel too proved right, as she generally was.

'Didna we tell you about the marriage settlement? And were we not to be trusted to mak' everything as siccar as law and auld Dauvit Milne and that laddie Dalgleish, Teeny Carstairs' man, could bind them? As for any story at this time of the day about auld Drysdale's living longer than Maggie Craig's mother, because he was in Scotland and she was in India, it's perfect havers on the face o't—more than that, it's clean profanity, as if death couldna travel faster than the earth and the sun either, and do his work as sune here as there. We may dismiss that lee. No that I'm for a minute evening your worthy father to be a leear, Clary, my dear,' Miss Janet condescended to correct herself. 'Everybody kens he is a maist respectable man. But men, begging your pardon, Lieutenant, are simple, and it stands to nature that they will believe what suits their purpose, though it's as wild a ferlie as ever set up an auld ballant. So, Lieutenant, you micht have been a bleacher and dyer in your ain person instead of an offisher in her Majesty's service, but I think you and Clary will agree with me that you're better as you are—you'll allow we did the best for you.'

"'Deed did we,' chimed in Miss Bethia; 'and now you'll get your portion back again, like Joseph—or was it Benjamin?—and Clary, here into the bargain.'

THE END.

BILLING AND SONS, PRINTERS, GUILDFORD.

CPSIA information can be obtained
at www.ICGtesting.com
Printed in the USA
BVHW022340011222
653288BV00009B/142

9 781164 917168